Twice to St David's

David W. James

GOMER

First edition—1995

ISBN 1 85902 149 2

© David W. James

Printed by J. D. Lewis & Sons Ltd,
Gomer Press, Llandysul, Dyfed

For
Mary, Ann and Richard

ACKNOWLEDGEMENTS

It is twelve years since *St David's and Dewisland* was published. In the acknowledgements to that book there was a long list of those without whose help it would never have been published. They contributed their memories and living voices. And they remain 'the cloud of witnesses' whose memories or presence and ready help have made possible a 'second pilgrimage' to this historic parish and to a city that will soon be given a charter confirming its official status as city from the hands of Her Majesty the Queen. Older and younger chroniclers are still active. Glyn Walters and Dewi Rowlands continue to make alive the old characters and old words and customs that otherwise would be forgotten; Nona Rees is wrapped in the history of the cathedral and the Saints; Peter Davies has dug deep into the history of farms and old families; and (more recently) W. J. (Bill) Rees has brought a wider and less local historical view to bear. It has been a privilege and a pleasure to have learnt from them all.

I am immensely grateful to those who willingly and generously helped in the process of assembling photographs. Thanks to Nona Rees, Terry John and Philip Clarke; to the Dean and Chapter of St David's Cathedral; the National Library of Wales; Royal Commission on the Ancient and Historical Monuments of Wales; to Mary John of the Regional Library in Haverfordwest, and to Anita Harries; to Ruth Barker and her mother; Mevin Thomas; J. T. Davies; Jenny Thomas; Elsie Griffiths; Barbara Thorne of Mathry School; Dewi Rowlands; John Williams; Mike Plant of Lower Treginnis (and Farms for City Children); and to Christopher Taylor at The Bookshop for his help with checking proofs of the book.

Lastly, my sincere thanks to Gomer Press: to Mr John Lewis for a warm welcome and acceptance; to Mrs Mairwen Prys Jones, whose task it was to correct the manuscript, to assemble the photographs, and finally with care and patience to nurse it into publication; and to all others in Gomer Press who had a part to play in the final printing and publication.

My thanks to all.

CONTENTS

Evensong

The grey liquid light of a damp winter afternoon was fading fast, and the alcoves of this cathedral library, high up in a north tower that once housed Treasury and Chapter House, were already pockets of gloom. All that remained of light came from the east window, a shy softness, a narrow strip along its length. Four o'clock, time of evensong, was very near, the volunteer librarians were tidying up, and it was time for me to go, and leave again my long and endless task of gathering together things found scattered, nuggets of long ago, in the old volumes of this treasure-house, fabric material that would eventually and hopefully be woven into a little tapestry history of this parish and its cathedral church. Down the worn steps, then, of the staircase within the tower walls, down to the north aisle, and then, for some unknown reason, across the presbytery, past the tomb of Edmund Tudor, past the parclose screen, and across to the somewhat lighter south aisle, on my way down the nave and over to the north door.

It came out of the gloom and caught me on my way through the arched doorway of the presbytery. From the choir from the gloom a human voice reciting the words of evensong. The voice of one solitary priest, repeating words, or something like the same words, that had echoed within these walls for eight hundred years, throughout the length of this unique cathedral's Norman history, perhaps for hundreds more. A lone priest talking to himself, and to his God; a tiny mortal doing his duty, to himself, and to his church, alone or almost alone in a vast and darkening sacred house, in an indifferent world.

Cathedral, like monastery, has its rules, its set services, its ritual, that must be kept and spoken or sung at fixed times to a congregation of hundreds, or one, or none.

It was strange, eerie. Unforgettable. A voice and a form of words tying today with a long distant past. So, said T. S. Eliot's *Little Gidding*,

> So, while the light fails
> On a winter's afternoon, in a secluded chapel
> History is now.

1

Music for St David's Day.
London Welsh Chorale (conductor Kenneth Bowen), 29 February, 1992.
(Photograph copyright Frank Menger 1992)

2

That priest was not alone. Something, and not for the first time, stirred.

History, said Eliot, is now. Here is St David's. Here is the cathedral. When we walk towards its plain grey outside and then enter into its peace and beauty, we become consciously or unconsciously linked with a past of thirteen hundred years that has seen victory and defeat, joy and disappointment, richness and poverty, and change, always change. But one thing has not changed: the fact that Dewi Sant the Saint, the monk, with his few companions began his work here, lived here, walked this land and died here. And T. S. Eliot springs to mind again, lines this time from *Murder in the Cathedral*, performed more than once in this very building. Below the Library is the Chapel of St Andrew, rebuilt by Bishop Gower, but dedicated to St Thomas a Becket, who was murdered in Canterbury in 1170.

And those lines—

Wherever a saint has dwelt . . .
There is holy ground, and the sanctity shall not depart from it
Though armies trample over it, though sightseers come with guide-books looking over it . . .
From such ground springs that which forever renews the earth.

History was at evensong. History is now when the past comes into the present. Here in St David's, or in Canterbury.

3

The Saint

No-one doubts that a man whose name was Dewi (or David) came to this place now called after him, established a monastery here, became a great evangelical preacher, 'the rule and model of right living', and eventually Patron Saint, the Dewi Sant of the Welsh. And there is very little else that we know about him. In spite of this we do know that because of some awareness, some emotional or intellectual or national awareness, some feeling, he became revered in that strange thing, the heart of the nation. His memory was retained through times of national forgetfulness, his good works were somehow remembered, the image grew, and he emerged and was accepted as Patron Saint.

'Dewi Sant'—Llanddewibrefi.

4

Out of that little we know of him, we (helped perhaps by the poets) created the image of a man, presumably of noble bearing and of great height, someone worthy of remembrance even to this day.

It is said that within forty or fifty years after his death Patrick was forgotten in Ireland; the awareness that eventually made the Irish think of him as Patron Saint came centuries later. So it was with Dewi Sant. We know that his name was sufficiently well known to be included in the Catalogue of the Saints of Ireland, drawn up about 730 A.D. Another manuscript, again Irish, of some seventy years later tells us that his monastery was called Mynyw and that his festival fell on the first day of March. A manuscript from Brittany tells us that he was a pupil of Illtud and was known as 'the Waterman' because of his strict mode of life. Asser, abbot of St David's who because of his learning was called to the court of King Alfred, mentions David's name and his monastery. Then towards the end of the ninth century his name appears five times in a poem called 'Armes Prydein Fawr'. Here he is recognised as a champion of the church, and as such he is asked to join with three great military leaders of the past to unite the Celtic nations and to drive the Saxon English into the sea. The unknown bard or cleric knew of the oppression that the Welsh had endured from the Saxons under Athelstan their king and others. He wanted his people freed. And he wanted Dewi, great leader of the church, to lead the crusading armies alongside their military leaders, his holy banner in the lead. In other words, he wanted Dewi to fulfil his role as national leader, and he would not have brought him in had he known that the name and reputation of the Saint had slipped from the mind and memory of his countrymen. Dewi, after all, had been dead for three hundred years.

A century or so after the time of 'Armes Prydein', in 1081, William the Conqueror made his surprise visit. In 1093 Rhys, Prince of Deheubarth and patron prince of the cathedral, was killed fighting the Normans. And in that eleventh century the monastery was ravaged six times. Somewhere around that time, according to the Life of Caradog, a monk came to St David's and had to cut his way through a wilderness of briars to reach the shrine. Three years before the death of Rhys, Rhygyfarch of Llanbadarn had foreseen disaster and had written

5

the first Life of the Saint. That Latin Life was followed about a century later by another Latin Life, compiled by Gerald of Wales, and in yet another century came the Welsh Life by the Anchorite of Llanddewibrefi.

Rhygyfarch's eleventh century Life praised the sanctity of David, listed his miracles and good works, and described the workings of his monastery. But the great aim of Rhygyfarch's Life was to magnify the greatness of the Celtic Church to which he and his father Sulien, twice bishop, belonged. Rhygyfarch knew that that Church was facing annihilation with the approach of the Normans. To try to save the monastery and the Celtic Church he had to praise the founder of the monastery.

It was another thirty years before the Normans imposed an alien bishop on St David's. In their practical wisdom and foresightedness and self-interest they then built their cathedral on the site of St David's monastery. They paid that degree of respect to a site that was as remote as it was illogical. But that imposed Norman edifice became itself a guarantee of the permanence of the legend of David, a safer guarantee without doubt, ridiculous as it may seem, than would have been the memory of the Welsh. It was placed in the hands of Canterbury and of Rome. And in the time of Bernard, the first Norman bishop (1115 to 1147), the cult of David was recognised by Pope Calixtus II; strictly a recognition and not a canonisation of the founder. In 1389 it was decreed that the feast of St David should be observed by the province of Canterbury. And in 1415, a century after Bishop Henry Chichele of St David's was translated to the archbishopric of Canterbury, another directive was issued increasing the dignity of the ceremonial to be observed.

All this belonged to the medieval and Anglican Church. It tells us nothing of how David was remembered in Wales in general and in the minds of the country-folk. But there is one glimmer of light. Five centuries after 'Armes Prydein Fawr', Dafydd Llwyd of Mathafarn near Machynlleth wrote a long poem on very much the same lines. Richard III was on the English throne, and Wales (or more particularly the poets) throbbed with rumours that Henry Tudor, grandson of Owen Tudor of Penmynydd in Anglesey, was on the point of coming out of exile and landing in Wales. Henry Tudor was descended from the Welsh Princes, had Welsh blood in his veins (some say that he hadn't, but whether he had or not was entirely beside

The shrine—Niche and modern Reliquary, Trinity Chapel.

the point—the Welsh believed he had), and win for himself the throne of England. Dafydd Llwyd, like the anonymous author of 'Armes Prydein', lived in hope of this, exulted in the hope, made a stirring call for Welsh support, and asked that 'all of our race, every district' should work 'for David'. Once again the Patron Saint was asked to be a leader of his nation against oppression and for freedom.

Henry VIII followed Henry Tudor on the English throne. Then came the Reformation, the break with Rome, and the appointment of William Barlow as the first reforming Protestant bishop of St David's. Barlow attempted to destroy St David's and the reputation of the Saint. He called the place 'a barbarous dangerous corner' (of the country). The high eminence of the Saint was in danger, and the place ceased to be a great centre of pilgrimage.

Pilgrimage to St David's and everywhere else in this country ended, then, with the Reformation. Bishop Ferrar, it is said, destroyed all the cathedral service books. That was that. But pilgrimage, unofficial and on a smaller scale did not cease, here or anywhere else. And when 'the declension and decline' of religious enthusiasm came over the country there came the rise of Dissent and the Methodist Revival. That Revival led to a great resurgence not only of religious but of national fervour, a great demand for education, and the awakening of the spirit of radicalism.

The Saint's Feast Day continues to be a time for celebration, but even that special occasion is now secularised beyond belief. There remains one assured fact. The poets remember him. Saunders Lewis, Gwenallt, Waldo Williams, James Nicholas— they have written their odes and *awdlau* to Dewi Sant, and have found inspiration in him in times of crisis and of danger. On and around the Saint's Day are our contemporary usuals—the dinner, the lecture, the eisteddfod, the concert, the *cymanfa ganu*, drama, children wearing the national costume, eulogy, brief remembrance. The poets, as is expected of them, go deeper. When the language is threatened, when there is some threat to the land of Wales: whenever these cast their dark shadows, as they do, then our poets, following the anonymous writer of 'Armes Prydein' and Dafydd Llwyd, turn to our patron Saint, turn to all the imagery associated with his name, and ask for help.

The Place

St David's was a borough in Norman times. It has also been called a village and a town, this gathering of houses and farms that never in its history, except for some fifty years in the last century, had a population of more than two thousand. It has a cathedral that is different from all others, and because of that has been called a city, by reputation and respect and not by charter. That was the verdict of the centuries. Then on 7 July 1994 the Prince of Wales made a momentous announcement, that by gift of Her Majesty the Queen, St David's was to be officially recognised as a city, as was Armagh in Ireland.

St David's for most of its time has heard two languages, which does not mean that it was always bilingual. Here for a long time there have been two populations, that of the country Welsh, and that of town or city, then and now more English than not. It sits on a peninsula of great historical and geological interest, ringed by a marvellous coast. Here uniquely is that cathedral hidden in a hollow, far away from the centre of what was once a vast and unwieldy diocese. Here was and still is an ancient place of pilgrimage. Here today is an active place, full of busy-ness and no great employment, a place that for its size has carried a ridiculously large amount of history and prestige.

The Cathedral from the Bishop's Palace.

9

Here have lived people who have been as fond of the sea as of their windswept and stony land. Here there never was a mansion of the country gentry, and no castle of a conquering race. The castle of this place was its cathedral, and to that cathedral precinct at one time came kings and archbishops, and chancellors of the older universities and of their country, England, and where lived a bishop who was lord marcher and in whose hands was the power of life and death. And remarkably it is a place that owes almost all to a Welshman, a monk but a man of princely ancestry, of whom we know little except that he brought the Christian religion with him and preached a revival of that religion, and built here a monastery and made the place famous in its day. A man of commanding personality and stature whose image emerged and faded and re-emerged in the minds and hearts of his countrymen, finally and with the help of others to become the Patron Saint of Wales.

How did it all begin? When and why did he ever come to this particular corner of west Wales?

According to the Life of the Saint, his father was Sant, son of Ceredig, prince of Ceredigion (which is Cardigan), and he was divinely ordered to go down to the ancient kingdom of Dyfed. There he ravished a girl called Non, daughter of a half Irish local chieftain.

The boy David grew up 'full of grace and lovely to behold'. After completing his education he travelled all over southern Wales and England founding monasteries, and eventually came, or returned, to Hen Vynyw, a monastery, now an attractive church not far from Aberaeron. Then in the fullness of time he and three of his most faithful companions came to a place called Vallis Rosina, which is the valley of the river Alun here in St David's.

What were they looking for? In the words of Gerald of Wales the holy men who settled here 'chose purposely such a retired habitation to avoid the noises of the world, and preferring an heremetical to a pastoral life, they might more freely provide for that part which shall not be taken away.' They were looking for a place where they could live in peace and nurture the spiritual, the life within. And that is what they found in the Valley.

Ever since that sixth century, time of David, men and women from many countries have followed their example and come to

The river Alun, Domus juxta Pontem, St Nicholas Penffos. *c.* 1895.
('Tŵr Bach' to the locals).

St David's: the Saints of old from Ireland and Brittany, pilgrims, kings and queens and prelates, the curious and the devout, the holidaymakers and the pilgrim tourists of today. Most come and go, and come again. Many stay. And all presumably are looking for something that is different, in surroundings of peace and beauty where, in the words of Jan Morris, one feels 'the hush that is the unmistakable pause of holiness.'

Rhygyfarch wrote his *Life* of David to keep alive the memory of the Saint and of the Celtic Church. He tells the story of his birth, his miracles, his monastery, his elevation to supremacy —and his death.

> And so his body, carried in the arms of holy brethren, and accompanied by a great throng, is honourably committed to the earth and buried in his own monastery. But his soul without any limit of passing time is crowned for ever and ever.

The Celtic Church disappeared with the coming of the Normans, who built the cathedral for their own purposes. And the great age of medieval pilgrimage began. Had that simple act of burial in his own monastery not taken place here, then the legend of the man and the saint, and indeed all that has been

11

notable in the history of this place, would never have happened. And there would have been no pilgrimage.

That is why they came, and continue to come, pilgrims and sightseer pilgrims, to this church in the hollow, that, in the words of H. V. Morton, 'possesses the longest memory in Britain.'

The Pilgrim's Dream

A pilgrim is a man with a journey on his mind. St Paul told his converts that they were all 'strangers and pilgrims' on this earth; and John Bunyan turned the pilgrimage of life into the allegory of his *Pilgrim's Progress*. The idea of pilgrimage dominated the mind and mood of those early pilgrims in the third and fourth century who began the great flood of medieval pilgrimage which nearly ended with the Reformation. Nearly. Pilgrimage, individually or in the mass, remains, is and always has been a significant element in all the great religions of the world.

Medieval man made his confession to the priest, who gave him the absolution that removed his guilt, but not the impending punishment in purgatory or in hell. To remove or reduce this punishment he had to do something, and one of the things he could do was to go on pilgrimage. He could travel to the Holy Land, to see and touch the places where Christ had lived and worked and died. Or he could go to Rome in search of the places and the relics that belonged to St Peter and St Paul. After Jerusalem and Rome came Santiago de Compostella in Spain, where he could see and touch the marvellous relics of St James. Then this urge to go on pilgrimage grew and spread, so that most of the countries of Europe established shrines that were dedicated to their native saints. That is how St David's emerged. The pilgrim to St David's could see and touch here the bones of a Celtic Saint, see the places that tradition has connected with his life, and in pre-Reformation days look at those relics that William Barlow (the first Protestant bishop of St David's) was to dismiss contemptuously as 'two heads of silver plate enclosing two rotten skulls stuffed with petrified clouts; item, two arm bones, and a worm-eaten book covered with silver plate'. And then the pilgrim could push his gifts through one of the three niches on the north side of the shrine, and go home, his conscience eased.

Pilgrimage became a trade. It brought wealth to the shrines, and all kinds of problems. It led to a shortage of relics, which in turn led to all kinds of manipulations and deceptions. Then there was the problem of those who had neither the wealth nor the physical strength to go to Palestine or to Rome. This led directly to the multiplication of alternative shrines. St David's became an alternative shrine when Pope Calixtus the Second confirmed that pilgrims who travelled twice to St David's were reckoned to have done the equivalent of having gone once to Rome. For the first time our cathedral church was called the Church of St Andrew and St David; and the profitable business of pilgrimage to it had been encouraged in a most ingenious way.

One of the more notorious aspects of the pilgrim trade, which contributed much to its demise, was the sale of indulgences. To be able to pay for an indulgence, a certificate of exemption from doing penance or from going on pilgrimage, meant in the end a reduction of expensive journeys overseas, an easy way out. The sale of indulgences inevitably grew rapidly, for obvious reasons, until that memorable day when Martin Luther challenged the trade and, in 1517, pinned his 95 theses to the church door in Wittenburg.

The Presbytery ceiling.

14

With the Reformation, and Henry VIII''s break with Rome, came the end of medieval pilgrimage in its organised form, but pilgrimage of a less institutionalised kind continued. As Chaucer's fourteenth century pilgrims had gone to Canterbury, all thirty-one of them like a holiday crowd, so today the thousands that come to St David's, year after year, are also pilgrim tourists or trippers. They walk the land that St David walked, they enjoy the beauties of coastal path and beach, and they make for the cathedral—amble through its nave and aisles and chapels, read the documented monuments, and gaze at the architectural loveliness of nave and chapel and Bishop's Palace. The medieval pilgrim came to his shrine afraid of the punishments of purgatory and of hell; he gained consolation from touching the tangibles of religion, the relics of his saint. He stood in awe. So, more casually, does the modern pilgrim tourist. He too stands and looks in awe. It is all a matter of degree. Some aspects of religious respect remain.

To deepen the sense of reverential awe in the minds of simple and illiterate men and women of the Middle Ages, to help soothe their frail minds and bodies—that was the great aim of the pilgrim centres. And it depended on the belief that the efficacy and power of the saint's holy life had been transferred to his relics. David had come and worked and lived and died in his *llan* in St David's. His relics were here. So were those of Justinian, his confessor, and of Caradog. The magnetism to the medieval mind lay in those relics.

The initial story of England's greatest centre of pilgrimage, Canterbury, where in 1170 Thomas a Becket was murdered by four knights in front of his altar, is comparatively straightforward. Almost immediately the crowds were making their way to the tomb of this 'Archbishop and Martyr' in the cathedral's Trinity Chapel. St David's belonged to a much older age. In his story there is more legend, less fact, and very little hard evidence of the growth in numbers of pilgrims to his shrine. But there is another cathedral that has a closer link with St David's, and a greater clutter of legend. Glastonbury is a world apart.

It is said to be the oldest Christian centre in England. It started with a little church built on the lower reaches of Glastonbury Tor, the high hill that overlooks what was once swampy land occasionally flooded by the tidal waters of the Bristol Channel. There is nothing much to go by, they say, except that that early church was a Celtic monastery founded by monks from Wales or from Ireland and supported in later years by the royal house of Wessex. Then in the twelfth century the monks of Glastonbury decided to compile their own history of the monastery from the beginning to the time of Duncan, who became abbot in 940.

The legends of Glastonbury began there: that Christianity was first brought to England by Joseph of Arimathea, sent over by Philip the Apostle, and that he had founded a religious community in Glastonbury; that St Patrick had visited it, and St David, and St Bridget; even that the young Jesus, in the 'missing years' of New Testament history, had come there and built a chapel with his own hands.

As pilgrims were not easily satisfied with stories of saints' visits, Glastonbury went ahead and claimed that Joseph of Arimathea had died there and lay buried on the slopes of the Tor; that Patrick and David had died there, and lay buried there; and that the bones of Aidan, bishop of Lindisfarne, had been brought there for safe keeping. Pilgrims wanted relics, Glastonbury wanted bones. The monks gave their firm assurance that the bones of all these monks lay within their boundaries. The pilgrims believed the monks, and Glastonbury became a great centre of pilgrimage.

There were other claims, made this time not by monks but by William of Malmesbury, and reported by Gerald of Wales. These were that the monks had discovered within the bounds of the monastery the burial place of King Arthur and his second wife, Guinevere. William of Malmesbury claimed that Avalon (the Welsh Ynys Afallon, the legendary Celtic land of perpetual youth where all great warriors found their final resting place) was not an island in the western oceans but this flat land around Glastonbury. And that King Arthur, mortally wounded in the battle of Camlan, had been brought to Glastonbury and buried in its holy soil. This was then linked with the legend of the Holy Grail, said to have been the cup used in the Last Supper and brought over by Joseph of Arimathea. The legend went on to say that Joseph buried it in an unknown place near the Tor, and this began another legend, the Quest of the Holy Grail, by King

16

The collapsed cromlech, Coetan Arthur, on Carn Llidi.

Arthur's Knights of the Round Table, and by many in times since.

There are place-names in St David's that remind us of King Arthur—Penarthur, the farm; and Coetan Arthur on Carn Llidi. More illuminating is the reference to Glastonbury in Rhygyfarch's *Life*. David, he said, his education and apprenticeship completed, went on a great missionary journey across South Wales and as far as north-east England. On that journey he founded twelve monasteries to the praise of God. And the first of these was Glastonbury. It is no wonder, then, that since the eighth century Glastonbury claimed 'the blessed David' as one of its patrons. And, typical of its ardent propaganda, it also claimed his bones.

Legends are legends; not history, but a backcloth to history. Medieval pilgrims swallowed legends whole. They believed in them. They saw legends as the colour of pilgrimage.

Glastonbury has its rich store of legends. St David's by comparison is less richly endowed. There are legends of the Saints of Brittany and Ireland; there was heavy traffic between the churches of the Western Seas. And the pilgrims came to St David's in their thousands. George Owen of Henllys in the

17

time of Queen Elizabeth I wrote of what he had heard—that the moneys collected in the chapels of the coast (in particular, St Justinian), moneys given in gratitude for safe landings and moneys given in hope of a safe journey home, were in such quantities that they were shovelled into buckets on the Friday to be counted in the cathedral on the Saturday.

Ours normally were humbler visitors. But medieval kings and queens did come to St David's, not always in the dress of pilgrims. And there have been many Royal visits in this century, and a massive pilgrimage to celebrate the sixteen hundredth anniversary of the Council of Nicaea as well as many other more local pilgrimages. In 1963, the Chapel of St Mary's College was restored to become a centre of pilgrimage. When the curious and the devout came in the latter half of the nineteenth century they found this chapel roofless, a gaping wound. They come today, the devout and the curious, from America and Scandinavia and Europe and the Far East. They can stand by the West Door inside the cathedral and lift their eyes towards the High Altar and the glories of its ceilings. They can walk the headland, grey rock and heather and gorse. They can see beauty all around them, and they can find what the pilgrim throughout the years had yearned for, a sense of peace.

For wherever a Saint has dwelt,
There is holy ground, and the sanctity shall not depart from it.

City, Circle, Cross

It was Henry James, the American novelist, who said that you can't see the pattern in the carpet when you're lying face down on it. And that is true in other matters, in, for instance, the lay-out of country or town or village. You must see things from above. Here in St David's are lines and patterns that have been here for fifteen hundred years. Modified, used or neglected, hidden in part, they have been and still are here, trimmed by the working of the centuries, visible only from above.

Overlooking the Square, the old Market Square or Cross Square (the square that is in fact a triangle, the old open space or village green where fairs and public meetings were once held), is a fourteenth century cross, a pedestal with six steps and a tapered column. At its head is a Celtic Cross, placed there in 1873, a stone circle resting between two imposed crosses, overlooking the meeting of the city's streets and facing The Pebbles and Tower Gate and the cathedral. The original cross was broken a long time ago, and the story is that one half of it can be seen cemented into the courtyard wall of the big house of Treleddyn away towards the west, and the other half lost somewhere within the vaults under the Bishop's Palace. Immediately below the Cross is the Memorial Garden built after the Second World War, surrounded by a stone wall capped with sea-washed stones. And in this wall, roughly circular in shape, are four stout entrances facing the four points of the compass. They are linked by two diagonal pathways and where they cross stands the flagpole. There is nothing unusual in this lay-out until an aerial photograph reveals the secrets of its design. The surrounding wall is a circle; the two pathways, diameters, are the arms of a cross. The Memorial Garden is in the shape of a Celtic Cross lying flat on the ground.

The story doesn't end there. The cathedral lies uniquely in a hollow, it is cruciform in shape, it lies on a slope, and around it lie the broken remains of an ancient Close Wall, whose design is hidden by the geography of the place.

It was in a narrow steep-sided part of the Valley, the Vallis Rosina 'which the Britons called Hodnant', that David and his three disciples lit their first fire in the name of the Lord. Some seven hundred and fifty years later the Close Wall was built around cathedral, Bishop's Palace, the colleges, the houses of the precentor and the four archdeacons, all grouped alongside a bisecting stream and joined by a little bridge.

To the west lay some high and protective ground. From that natural bulwark two protective arms of the wall were built to surround the 'city' and to come together above the Thirty Nine Steps in a gateway that became the main entrance into the Close. That gateway is one of four entrances set in the surrounding wall that, considering the lie of the land, is as near circular as possible. The four are linked by a medley of road and pathway, diagonally, and these meet by the entrance to the Bishop's Palace. They are the arms of the cross, and face the four points of the compass, north and south and west and east, like the gateways of the Memorial Garden. Like that Memorial Garden the pattern of the Close incorporates a circle and a cross. The pattern is revealed.

Patterns and images carry meanings, and this pattern of circle and cross, whose repetition can hardly have been an accident, carries layers of historic and symbolic meaning that relate directly to the history of early Celtic Christianity and at the same time explain the original development of St David's.

The Celtic Church was a church of seafarers, its strongholds Cornwall and Brittany, Ireland, the Isle of Man, and northwestern Scotland. The Lives of the Saints tell us that 'it was good and godly to go on pilgrimage to holy places', and these holy places were scattered along the western seaboard, and the only way to get to them was by sea. St David's (or whatever it was called in those early days) became of immense significance because it was situated on the crossing point for all these lines of communication. The early monastery was built in the Valley behind the headland, and on either side of this Valley lay the little landing places for these pilgrims, at Porth Glais, St Justinian's, and Porth Mawr, which is the Whitesands of today.

Two of the Close Wall gates were directly linked with these little landing places and with the seafaring Christianity of the early Saints. Porth Padrig (St Patrick's Gate), now a broken arch, looked towards Porth Glais and Cornwall and Brittany. Face that rough climb from the Bishop's Palace to Penporth Gwyn (the White Gate, although nothing of it is left to remind you) and you will stand on the spot where Henry II of England, returning from Ireland in 1172 through Porth Mawr, met the canons of the cathedral and moved in procession with them to the cathedral church, habited like a pilgrim, as Gerald of Wales tells us, and leaning on a staff.

The other two gates are different in that they belonged to the old land routes. Of Bonyng's Gate hardly a stone remains. The newly furbished road from the Palace passes the archdeacons' houses and the old Treasury and the Canonry and glides past it unawares and comes to Pont y Penyd, the Bridge of Penance. Once across the bridge over the Alun the modern road turns right for Quickwell Hill. But the old road went straight on and climbed a hedged lane to meet the coast road going north from the city. This was the old Feidr Dywyll, the Dark Lane, the road followed by old pilgrimages from the north, from Bardsey Island, which is Ynys Enlli, and Llanfaes near Brecon, and Llanbadarn Fawr. It was the old pilgrim road to and from the north. Old John Ogilby had it on his sketch map for St David's and the north. There was no other. A mile or so from the city it entered a part of the parish that remains full of strangely suggestive names—Pont y Gwrhyd (Bridge of the Fathom) near the legendary Capel y Gwrhyd; Waun y Beddau (the field of the graves); Tre-prior; Yr Hen Fynwent (the old graveyard); all alongside Dowrog Moor, once called Tir-y-Pererinion (land of the pilgrims) and granted, so it is said, by Rhys ap Tewdwr 'for the use of Pilgrims making their devotions to St David's'. Some say it was part of an old Roman road called Fleming's Way. And it was the road taken by Archbishop Baldwin and Gerald of Wales on their preaching crusade of 1188. After leaving St David's they stopped at Nevern, then on to Cardigan, sleeping the night at St Dogmael's Abbey and being entertained next day at Cardigan Castle by the Lord Rhys, then on to Emlyn (Newcastle Emlyn), keeping well to the north of the Preseli Hills, and then to Strata Florida or Ystrad Fflur. Gerald gives the stopping places and no more.

The last of the four entrances to the Close, Tower Gate, remains a majestic ruin, the main entrance and the gateway most often used by the pilgrim tourists of today who come along the M4 and the Severn Bridge. It was also the main gateway for the second and medieval great age of pilgrimage that extended from the coming of the Normans to the Reformation. This gate faces east towards Carmarthen: on that route are Llawhaden, one of the seven bishop's palaces of old, and Whitland, Hendy-gwyn ar Dâf. And in its length lies more than one hospitium or resting place for sick and tired pilgrims. Most notable is Llanfihangel Abercywyn with its medieval pilgrims' tombstones and the remains of a hospice that is still called 'Pilgrim's Rest'. This was, and still is, the road along which kings and queens and prelates came on their way to the shrine of David. And when they arrive they walk through Tower Gate, as has always been the way of pilgrims.

It is clear, then, that the significance of St David's in the days of the Celtic Church and in Norman-English times is graphically mirrored in the shape and structure and the symbolism of what is on Cross Square and inside the Cathedral Close, that is, the circle and the cross.

The significance of the Celtic Cross is also marked inside the church. At the west end of the nave have been gathered certain large stones (found on nearby farms) that will eventually be

Incised slab (bottom left) once used as a gate-post on Penarthur farm.
The drawing is dated 1867.
(Reproduced by kind permission of Haverfordwest Library)

22

placed in a lapidarium under St Mary's Hall. Each carries an incised cross in its simplest form. There are others cemented into the faces of chapel altars. There is the memorial stone to the sons of Abraham, the bishop who was slaughtered by the Northmen in 1087: this carries the same design in a more ornate form. Whether simple or ornate, this design, incorporating a circle and a cross, was the trademark of the early Christians from the fifth to the seventh century. Its message is historical and symbolic. If the cross was the sign of Christianity, what was the circle?

The symbolism of the circle was dear to the heart of Joseph Campbell, the American who wrote the *Power of the Myth*, a study of primal society and its mythology. The whole world is a circle. The circle is totality; it has no beginning and no end. To come nearer home, we know that the spiral and the circle were dear to the arts of the ancient Celts, and we believe that their leaders, the Druids, performed their pagan rites within circles of oak trees or stones. The same symbolism, perhaps with less religious significance, lies in the circle of stones built for the purpose within which the Gorsedd and the druids of today, the bardic fraternity of the National Eisteddfod, carry out their ceremonies.

There is something else. The early Christian missionaries dared not offend the pagan Welsh. To convert they had to persuade. And then, having won the initial battle of minds, they tactfully and carefully sanctified the wells and the circles that had been sacred to the Druids. The pagan well, sanctified, was then dedicated to a Christian Saint. And the Druidic sacred circle within its circle of stones or oak trees was sanctified when a Christian body was buried there, and a church built within its boundary. Hence the tendency to believe that early Christian cemeteries were surrounded by a mound or wall, the *llan* or boundary that only later took on the meaning of church. There is a circular burial place in the church of Clydau on the old road from St David's to Carmarthen, and much nearer home again in Llanhowel. Not far from St David's is Mathry church, built on a hill of great antiquarian interest. The churchyard is surrounded by a circular wall, and built into that wall, outside and to the right of the entrance gate, are two flat stones. Each is inscribed with a simple incised circle and cross.

23

To explain the circle and the cross as a symbol of the victory over paganism of the Christian religion, the cross imposed on the circle, may appear simplistic. There are other symbolic explanations. But that explanation of the pattern of circle and cross fits St David's because it is to be seen in the design of the Memorial Garden and plentifully in the design and contents of the Cathedral Close.

And it is a pattern on the ground that can best be read from above.

There are other circles or 'cylchs' in the history of the parish. These were administrative divisions of the parish organised in the early days of the cathedral church and discarded only in the 1930s. Each circle was called a 'cylch'—Cylch Mawr to the north, Cylch Bach to the south-east, Cylch Gwaelod y Wlad to the south-west, and Cylch y Dref.

There is yet another system of circles that must be visualised from above. It is a system of four concentric circles within which is illustrated all the history of St David's, city and parish, past and present. The first is that inner circle within which lies the beginning of its history, the monastic circle on which cathedral and Close were built. The second is the circle of town or city that grew up over the years around the Close. The third is that of the farmland, the ancient Celtic Welshery, its green grass growing to the very edge of houses and cathedral. And last, the encircling and once very busy coastline.

These four concentric circles remain clear-cut as they have been over the centuries. The life of cathedral and city, the life of the farm, and the activities of the little harbours—they have changed and continue to change. The circles remain.

Gerald of Wales

There are many reasons why Gerald of Wales must come into the story of St David's.

He was born in Pembrokeshire, in Manorbier, and there was some Welsh blood in his veins. He received his early education in this cathedral church of ours. He was vicar of Llanwnda, a lovely and very old church in the diocese down the coast from Fishguard, and held the prebend of Mathry, and was archdeacon of the cathedral. He wrote his *Itinerary through Wales* describing the journey on which he accompanied Archbishop Baldwin preaching the Third Crusade (1181), and came to St David's and described his stay. And he wrote his *Description of Wales*, in which he described the Welsh people and their characteristics, many of which are still evident today. And he loved and cherished this diocese, partly because of ambition, but for many other reasons as well. He travelled widely, but, wherever he was, St David's was not far from his mind. And, of course, he compiled the second *Life of St David*.

Gerald tried three times to become bishop of St David's. Twice he was nominated by the Chapter; three times he went to Rome to prosecute his appeal that the diocese should be freed from the yoke of Canterbury. He was offered Bangor and Llandaf. Nothing but St David's would do. He failed, and that is why the carved figure in Holy Trinity Chapel shows him with the mitre he never assumed lying at his feet.

Behind and beyond the ambition there was something else. He described himself as a Welshman, Gerallt Gymro, Gerald Cambrensis. 'I am sprung,' he said, 'from the Princes of Wales and from the barons of the Marches.' And that brings us to his family tree.

His grandmother was Nest, bright star of medieval Welsh romance and daughter of Rhys ap Tewdwr of the house of Dynefwr, last independent prince of Deheubarth and patron prince of the cathedral, and directly descended from that father figure of Welsh princes, Rhodri Mawr.

His grandfather was Gerald de Windsor, Norman governor of Pembroke Castle. One of the children of Gerald and Nest was David FitzGerald, who became bishop of St David's. Another was Angharad, who married William de Barri, a Norman noble. They had four sons, and the youngest of these was Gerald of Wales. He was therefore of mixed descent, the blood of the Welsh princes on the female side, that of the conquering and ruling Normans on the male side; an aristocracy created, as in so many other cases in the history of Wales, by marriage between male Norman and female Welsh.

Another of the children of Rhys ap Tewdwr was Gruffydd ap Rhys, and he was the father of Rhys ap Gruffydd, Lord of Cardigan Castle and Cilgerran Castle, and justiciar of South Wales appointed by Henry II to keep order amongst the Welsh princes. Gerald therefore was first cousin to the Lord Rhys. There is a monument to this great Welsh prince in the South Choir aisle of the cathedral. Right opposite, in the North Choir aisle, is another to his son, Rhys Grug. And in between the two, in Trinity Chapel, is the figure of Gerald.

Those were the princely associations that Gerald knew very well and of which he was immensely proud. The Welsh blood of those princes may have become thin in his veins, but he was, and told everybody that he was, passionately proud of his family and his country. He might well, had he had the chance, have fought for the liberty of Wales as he fought for the liberty of the diocese. He hated the Norman scheme of placing Norman bishops in Welsh sees.

Gerald knew why he failed. The English kings, Henry II and John, were worried over the insecurity of their control over Wales, fearing the power of the Norman barons and the Welsh princes. Had Gerald been appointed bishop, an office then of immense power, he would have had the backing of the Norman barons and the inherited support of the Welsh princes. An impossible situation.

He was a great character in his own right, a vibrant personality. What he told us about St David's is important. His valiant attempts to separate the diocese from Canterbury were important. The Church in Wales had to wait another seven hundred years to become disestablished. But although Gerald failed to become bishop, the Norman control over St David's that he tried to break became, ironically, the means whereby the cathedral and the diocese reached their peak in wealth and in significance. After all, the man who defeated him, Peter de Leia, was the man who built the cathedral.

The Giraldus Cambrensis niche in Holy Trinity Chapel.

Effigy of the Lord Rhys in the South Aisle.

Gerald died in 1223. Strangest of all is the fact that nobody knows where he died. It is possible that he breathed his last in the Menevia that he loved and never forgot.

There is one other reason why we should drag in this proud Norman into the story of St. David's.

The answer is devastatingly simple. Rhygyfarch's *Life* doesn't tell us that the Patron Saint was born in St David's. Neither does the Anchorite of Llanddewibrefi's Welsh version. Gerald the Welshman did. Whether or not David was born in this place is beside the point. The people of St David's were ready and willing to believe that he was.

Gerald of Wales had told them so.

Tudor Rose

'Welshmen shall not have castles'—that from one of Henry
IV's Statutes of Wales. Castles, in other words, were the
prerogative of the Norman conqueror. That was how Thomas
Pennant saw Caernarfon Castle—'That most magnificent
badge of our submission'. There is no castle in Dewisland, and
castles were, and are, symbols of the subjection of Wales. Some
will, let us be honest, say something similar about our cathedrals. St David's Cathedral was a Norman imposition, and the
Normans emphasised this when they designated it to St
Andrew first and then to St David. They subdued Dewisland
not by physical force but by means of religion. The bishop
became lord of the manor, and lord marcher, lord of life and
death. His cathedral became the powerhouse; his castle was the
cathedral. And buried underneath it were the dry bones of the
ancient Celtic Church. It was, nevertheless, a splendid imposition, now a priceless part of our Christian heritage.

The Normans built it, but it also true to say that it was the
bishops in Tudor times that finished it. The Tudor monarchs
were descended from Owen Tudor of Penmynydd in Anglesey;
and the marble monument to one of that blood, Edmund Tudor,
proudly announces the fact in the presbytery of the cathedral.

Henry VIII, first of the Tudors and son of Edmund Tudor, died
in 1509. And in that same year Edward Vaughan became bishop

Medieval (late 16th century) tiles on the floor of the sanctuary.

30

of St David's. It was he, last of the great builder bishops, who completed the cathedral. He added a third stage to the tower, covered in the open space between High Altar and the ante-chapel to create the Chapel of Holy Trinity, vaulted the eastern walk and the Lady Chapel, and connected Holy Trinity Chapel with the aisles by delicate stone screens, and for good measure restored St Justinian's Chapel on the coast. It was Edward Vaughan who gave prominence and wholeness to a cathedral that had hitherto been incomplete.

With Henry VIII came the Reformation and the dissolution of the monasteries. Edward VI carried on what his father had begun, and closed St Mary's College in 1549. That the cathedral church in St David's is the only cathedral in the country with a prebendal stall reserved for the reigning monarch is normally attributed to this dissolution, although there are other possible explanations. This prebendal stall belonged to the Master of the College, and with the dissolution it reverted to the Crown. The Royal Arms carried by the stall are attributed to Edward VI. It was also in the reign of Edward VI that William Barlow came as bishop.

In 1558 Elizabeth I ascended to the throne. In her reign the Bible was translated into Welsh, first by William Salesbury and then completely by William Morgan. Helping Salesbury were two men from the cathedral, Richard Davies, bishop, and Thomas Huett, precentor. The circulating schools and the Sunday Schools and the great religious revivals that were to come in the eighteenth and nineteenth century, and the resurgence of Welsh pride and nationalism that came with them—all were sparked into life by that translation of the Bible. Then in 1626 another great Welshman became Chancellor of the cathedral. Rhys Prichard wrote *Canwyll y Cymru*, the bases of Christian morality translated into doggerel verse, a book that had enormous influence on Welsh life and behaviour.

The Tudor Rose, carved and coloured, can be seen in all kinds of places in the cathedral. The symbolism of that Rose and the presence of Edmund Tudor's tomb in the presbytery—together they add something that is more native Welsh to this Norman edifice. Beyond all this, what was the significance of the Tudor reign to St David's? A Tudor monarch severed the link between St David's and Rome and its medieval heritage. Another Tudor monarch deprived it of St Mary's College. A Tudor queen made

The Royal Stall in the Choir.

the order that enabled illustrious Welshmen to give the nation its Welsh Bible. And one bishop under a Tudor monarch gave its wholeness and much of its beauty to the cathedral. And through the Tudors came Protestantism.

Unquestionably the greatest gift of the Tudor era was the Welsh Bible. Socially, spiritually, and educationally, the Welsh people grew into nationhood on the basis of that translation. Mention of education reminds us that those translators of the Bible, Salesbury, Davies, Huett, were all graduates of Oxford University. In 1566 Elizabeth I visited Oxford some time after a certain man had petitioned her to set up another college in the university. On 27 June 1571 letters patent of the Queen established Jesus College, the college of the Welsh. That petitioner happened to be Hugh Price, Treasurer of St David's Cathedral.

Princes, Prelates, Palace

The Palace lies to the west of the river Alun, a majestic ruin, perhaps more majestic in its present state than it was in its heyday. East of that river is the cathedral; and the precentor's house; the restored St Mary's Hall that was once the chapel of St Mary's College; and again towards the north the site or what remains of the vicars' choral quarters. And, strangely, the site of the Archdeacon of Carmarthen's house. Strangely, because the rest of the domestic accommodation lies on the west side, the Bishop's Palace side, the houses of the Archdeacons of St David's and Brecon, the site of the Archdeacon of Cardigan's house, long since gone, and the Chancellor's house, now the Canonry, and what was the Treasurer's house. Around all, east and west of the river, was once the Close Wall, the battlemented wall complete with its four gates. That was the original site, the original 'city' which was the 'civitas Kellmunnensis', the monastery of David.

The entrance stairs to the Palace Great Hall.

The cathedral was built to the greater glory of God. Would it be fair to believe that the Bishop's Palace, the great glory of the western and domestic side of the river, was built to the greater glory of human pride and power? Who built it and when?

The Celtic bishops, it is said, had a castle home on the high ground called Castell Penlan, overlooking the bishop's mill that once stood in the lower valley of the Alun. That great Celtic Age ended in utter desolation. Where then was the bishop's home?

The Normans came, and Bernard, the first Norman bishop of St David's. The Pope gave official recognition to the cult of David. Peter de Leia built the nave and choir, nucleus of the present cathedral, having demolished whatever was there before. And it was then that the medieval greatness of St David's began.

In a period of little more than one hundred years, from 1280 to 1389, are to be found the names of four illustrious bishops who held high office in councils of state and the highest rank in the church, and who are remembered in the history of St David's as the great builder bishops. They were Thomas Beck, who became bishop in 1280, David Martyn, Henry Gower, and Adam Houghton, a local man who died in office in 1389 and was buried within the precincts of his cathedral. Of these the most closely linked with the Bishop's Palace is Henry Gower, but it is likely that all four had a hand in the magnification of the palace whose ruins we look on in amazement today.

When the Normans built this church in Menevia, which was the old name for St David's, they were obliged to provide their bishops and the chapter and vicars choral, their own creation, with adequate domestic accommodation. In some instances they took their time. It was 1365 before Adam Houghton founded St Mary's College with its Master and seven priests with the intention of improving the musical standards of the cathedral. Two or three years earlier he had tried to see that his choristers and vicars choral were properly housed. And that was three hundred years after the time of Bernard. What accommodation was there for the bishop and his guests and pilgrim visitors? We do not know. Henry II came to St David's on his return from Ireland in 1172. According to Gerald of Wales he entered the Close by the White Gate, heard mass, supped, and went off to Haverfordwest. In 1188 Archbishop Baldwin came

North view of Cathedral and Palace, a painting by Pugin, c. 1790.
(Reproduced by kind permission of Haverfordwest Library)

36

to St David's, accompanied by Gerald. They were, he said, lodged by Bishop de Leia, and that was all. But there is some evidence that Henry II's visit had put Bishop David FitzGerald under some strain. The first royal pilgrimage on a grand scale, that of King Edward I and his queen, came in November 1284, and this made whatever inadequacies existed more obvious, and it is probable that the bishop of the time, Adam Houghton, had already begun to make improvements.

It took some two hundred years of reconstructing old buildings and adding new buildings to this bishop's area to bring things to the situation the remnants of which we see today, that is, from the time of Thomas Beck (end of the thirteenth century) to the time of Edward Vaughan (the beginning of the sixteenth century). Vaughan was the last of the builder bishops and the last bishop of St David's to be buried in his own cathedral. In between came Henry Gower, the man who, according to Richard Fenton's *Historical Tour of Pembrokeshire* (1810), was the 'avowed founder' of the Palace. Gower, he said, 'with a zeal proportionate to the dignity of the see and his own eloquent taste, was resolved to leave behind him a residence that would reflect lustre on his memory.' Fenton praises what we today appreciate most of all, the elegant porch with its flight of steps leading to the Great Hall, the rich mullions and tracery of that magnificent chamber, and most of all the arched parapet in chequered purple and yellow freestone. But Fenton ends with a note of seeming regret—whereas preceding bishops, men of high birth, had had the honour of entertaining kings there, Henry Gower had hoped to entertain the then reigning monarch Edward III (father of the Black Prince) and his Queen Philippa. They never came.

Was that the beginning of the end? Edward Vaughan added some beautiful elements to the fabric of the cathedral. But the country was becoming increasingly disturbed, its people and its clergy demoralised. And St David's suffered under a string of inefficient and uncommitted bishops. Then came the Reformation, and Edward Barlow, and the end of pilgrimage.

Barlow hated St David's, and must have hated the Palace. The much repeated story is that he stripped some of the lead from the roof of the Palace to provide his daughters with dowries. That is wrong. What he did was to deprive the Great Hall of its roof. He began the process of making the Palace useless as a residence, but did not demolish it. At least one other bishop came to live there, and parts of the building were still under cover when permission was granted to demolish it in 1616. Again it escaped, because a chapter meeting of 1633 was held within its walls. But as far as being an episcopal residence was concerned its days were over. Bishops during the latter half of the seventeenth century preferred to live in Brecon, and to be buried there. William Thomas, who became bishop in 1678, wanted to revive Barlow's plan to remove the see to Carmarthen, but Adam Ottley, who became bishop in 1713, did contemplate re-establishing the episcopal residence in St David's, despite the fact that he took residence in Abergwili and repaired the house and chapel there.

So the Palace became roofless, although some repairs were made during the time of cathedral reconstruction that was completed in 1877. The Palace became a hiding place for vandals and for squatting families, and a playground for children. 'Compared with the Palace,' wrote Eiluned Lewis in *The Captain's Wife*, 'all other playgrounds were dull and commonplace . . . leaving out consideration of its glorious past, of the prelates who lived like princes within its walls and entertained kings and noblemen in their feasts, the Palace was the best place in the world for Hide-and-Seek and every sort of game.' In the holes around the ruined walls were the nests of jackdaws. And the vaults, on which rested the dining halls of old, were wonderful places for playing Fox and Hounds. The largest episcopal palace in the country, a great and glorious piece of architecture, had become a playground.

Today it is well cared for, a splendid ruin, symbol of one-time wealth and pride, and of the medieval significance of the Close.

Bells

Bells communicate. They carry messages. Dewi Sant had a bell called Bangu that he rang when he tramped the countryside and called the people to worship. Bells, the single bell of the lonely country church, the ring of bells in the cathedral, they all make one of four announcements. They call to worship; they warn the people, as they did in wartime; they announce victory, of Easter Sunday or of some national success, triumph or joy; and in muffled tones they tell of death and mourning.

The Normans built their cathedral in the Valley and equipped it with bells and surrounded it with the walls of the Close. On the high ground to the east grew the medieval town or borough that has now become the official city of St David's. The bells carried messages from church to town. They linked the two communities.

Peter de Leia's cathedral was a cruciform structure with a stumpy central tower that presumably housed those bells. That tower collapsed towards the east in 1220. It was rebuilt, and in the fourteenth century, in the time of the greatest of builder bishops, Henry Gower, a second stage was added, and in the sixteenth century, in the time of Edward Vaughan, a third to complete the tower that we see today.

Why was the tower raised? Did it have something to do with the pilgrims? When they approached the sacred site, looking across the desolateness of Tretio Moor and Dowrog (Browne-Willis's 'Crug-glas-y-ddyfrog', the watery green hillock), they could see nothing of the cathedral. They could, when the second stage was added; and certainly could when the uplifted tower of Edward Vaughan completed the work; and then they forgot their aching limbs and gathered hope.

Or was it that the tower was extended upwards and the bells raised so that they would be more easily heard in the growing town and the surrounding countryside?

Gerald of Wales was acquainted with Peter de Leia's cathedral. But he was not very complimentary to Peter, nor had he cause to be. There were bells in the central tower, he said, but they were bad bells. The *Menevia Sacra*, compiled by Archdeacon Yardley in 1720 (but not published till 1927) said that at the beginning of the thirteenth century the bells were excellent. What caused the change we do not know. The collapse of the tower in 1220; the earthquake of 1284 that nobody knows much about—they must have damaged the bells. And the tower had to be rebuilt. It has been suggested that the octagonal tower of Tower Gate (dated the thirteenth century) was built then and used to accommodate the bells in the meantime. The second stage of the tower was furnished with a fine ring of bells.

There were five, cast or recast in a famous foundry in Bristol. And in addition there was another and smaller bell, used to announce the daily service.

The bells were raised when Edward Vaughan's third and overhanging stage was built, and one was added. That made a total of seven, the ring of six, and the 'sanctus' bell, which according to one of the vicars choral was 'debarred' from ringing with the others. About the middle of the seventeenth century two of these bells were stolen, a story told with relish by Richard Fenton but dismissed as inaccurate by later historians. By the eighteenth century things had worsened. Of the five bells that were there only two were whole. Manby in 1801 commented that it was doubtful whether the noise they made suggested joy or sorrow. In 1748 the four large ones became unfit for use. In 1765 they were ordered to be sold, and two new bells were cast, the one that is now on the cathedral tower, and a smaller one that, cracked, was disposed of in 1928. In 1856 the cathedral had three bells, two on the upper stage, one on the outside.

In 1862 Sir Gilbert Scott reported to the cathedral chapter on the precarious state of the tower; its foundation was sinking, helped by the weight of the bells. The tower and much of the nave then underwent the renovation that was completed in 1877. The bells had to wait until 1928. In that year a ring of eight bells, given anonymously, was cast for the cathedral by the Whitechapel foundry in London. They arrived in St David's in July of 1930, and were hung in the octagonal tower. That is their home today.

Some of the past remains. The sanctus bell is on the top of the cathedral tower. At the west end of the nave has been one of the three bells cast in the Bristol foundry between 1420 and 1480. It bears the inscription 'Soli Deo et Gratia'—'To God alone be the honour and glory'. All bells are christened, and named, like

40

Last of the medieval bells, now in the west side of the nave.

The Tower Gateway from 'The Little Steps'.

children, and have godparents. And the medieval base from which the bells were once hung is still in position in the upper section of the tower. As for the rest—where once they rang from the tower of a hidden cathedral in the Valley, they now ring out of the Octagonal Tower to the church hidden below, and over town and country. That Octagonal Tower sits on the boundary line between Close and city. The message, however, remains the same.

It is fair to assume, as the guide books so often suggest, that the early Celtic church in the Valley (how much rebuilding there was we do not know) had been built there for safety reasons, out of reach and hidden from the infidels and 'the gentiles'. That surely can not apply to the cathedral, as the guide books continue to suggest. When Peter de Leia was building his cathedral in 1181 the danger was over. The last Anglo-Saxon ravages had come in 1089. There were no more.

The new cathedral was being built, and the bells were rung to proclaim the fact. They still proclaim the presence of this cathedral, and also something else that is often overlooked. The cathedral is also the parish church. Whether those bells are always heard on the outer fringes of the parish is another matter.

Ffos y Mynach

'They say that . . .' are the opening words of the *Black Book of St David's*, the fourteenth century record of the bishop's lands. Old knowledge. The old characters knew where the boundaries were; and they knew because their forefathers knew. There were old pathways across the moors of St David's, linking farm with farm. They are now overgrown and lost, and only the 'old chroniclers' know where they were. They walked them.

One of these pathways, the longest in the parish, has now been cleared and signposted; time has bedded it well. And it is so old that no-one knows much about it.

Manby's *History and Antiquities of the Parish of St David's* (1801) says that it was nothing more than a roadway. He should have known it well: he lived in nearby Carnwchwrn. The *History and Antiquities of St David's* (Jones and Freeman 1856) discussed and described it over six pages and came to about the same conclusion. It is today, as it was then, something of a mystery. It runs right across the peninsula, roughly for nine miles, and roughly south to north. Starting by a little cove below Trelerw on the shore of St Bride's Bay, it keeps west of the pool on Dowrog Common, crosses the coastal road, and creeps up to end behind Carn Penbiri. Its Welsh name, *ffos*, is an indication that it was mostly a dyke, a trench or a ditch, or a mound raised to prevent flooding. There are two well-known farms alongside its path, Lower Harglodd, and Upper Harglodd, a farm once in the ownership of Sir James Hamilton, brother of Sir William (Emma's) Hamilton. Ask any local to explain Harglodd and he will cheerfully suggest that it is a corruption of 'ar glawdd', which means the top of a hedge or mound. In effect, this Ffos-y-Mynach, this Monk's Dyke, or, as Jones and Freeman had it, Ffos-y-Myneich, is a combination of both mound and dyke, a levelling of the ups and downs of the terrain to give a safe and level passageway across the peninsula.

It is certainly not a natural feature. It was man-made, by whom we do not know, and in consequence made to some purpose.

There is the possibility that it was nothing more than a road, a useful link between the coastal south and the coastal north.

44

There are some who regard it as linked with the famous sanctuary that Rhygyfarch's *Life* made so much about—'And let no kings or elders or governors, or even bishops or superiors or saints, dare to provide right of sanctuary in priority of holy David ... he provided right of sanctuary before every person ... because he is head and primate over all Britons.' Baring-Gould, one-time vicar of St Martin's in Haverfordwest, wrote a novel, *In Dewisland*, published in 1904. And he had his own explanation, which is as good as any. Cynyr of Caer Gawch, he said, gave his lands in Mynyw to the monks of the monastery. The monks then dug the trenches and threw up the banks to mark the boundary of their land and to keep their privacy. And Cynyr of Caer Gawch, we remember, was the father of Non, the mother of David. The dyke then would have marked a boundary and put some kind of limitation on the movements of the monks.

If Baring Gould was right, Ffos-y-Mynach had belonged to the monks of the Celtic monastery and long before Bernard became bishop in 1158. It was he who divided the parish into three (subsequently four) Circles or 'cylchs', for the better collection of tithes and the payment of prebends to the officers of the cathedral. The four areas were unequal in productivity, and the canons took them in turns. These four Circles remained part of the parish administration until the 1930s when with some other ancient parish customs they were discontinued. But it is significant that Ffos-y-Mynach marked the boundary between Cylch Gwaelod y Wlad and Cylch Mawr, and again between Cylch y Dre and Cylch Bychan.

On its way across the peninsula the dyke crosses some features of exceptional interest. The first going north from Trelerw is Dŵr Cleifion (waters of the ailing wounded). The little Bwdi stream, that runs into Caerbwdi on the coast of St Brides—the pebbled inlet below the remains of an old cornmill and a distinctively square limekiln—once flowed on to and across the road which is the back road from St David's to the airfield and a road of some significance: it was once the road to Middle Mill and to Haverfordwest. It is now culverted, and a very good spot from which to view the ups and downs of the dyke. It was here, at this ford, that, according to legend, the pilgrims washed their sore and dirty feet for the last time before entering on the last lap to the sanctuary of the cathedral.

The Ffos passes some well-known farms, Mynydd (Mwni) Du, once known as Pen-y-ffos, and Llangidige, a place-name that no-one has ever managed to explain. Not far away on the western fringe of Dowrog is Hendre Eynon, once a thatch-roofed and round chimneyed farmhouse where preachers of the Methodist Revival were warmly welcomed.

Around the northern end of Ffos-y-Mynach is that intriguing cluster of place-names, Treprior (the priory), Waun y Beddau; it is impossible to believe that they have no religious connection. And behind Penbiri, Eglwys y Cathau, a possible source of endless speculation. Beyond Penbiri again is legend—that Ffos-y-Mynach goes down to the north coast and then under the sea, to join with another on the further side of the Irish Channel.

At the north end of Dowrog is another Biblical place-name, Drws Gobaith (the doorway of hope), a metaphor for a departure from the gloom of the moor and a prospect of nearing the old coastal road to the north, the road of pilgrimage. Alongside Drws Gobaith, or more appropriately in its background, are the remains of 'tai unnos'. Whoever would manage to put up anything like a house in one night and get smoke pouring from its chimney by morning would claim the house for his own and the land beneath it.

Not far away is the largest standing stone in the parish, Maen Dewi, the stone of David. It may mark the burial place of some person of importance. More likely it was a marking spot, indicative of the trackway across the moor that we use today.

Without question the most interesting feature on this cross-country walk is Dowrog Moor or Common. It is larger than Trefaeddan Moor, or Tretio, it arouses a sense of mystery, it fascinates the naturalist, and it brings a gleam to the eye of the painter.

It is the largest of the many commons around St David's. It was historically a princely gift to the pilgrims, and the river Alun, which rises near Llangidige Fach, forms the link between it and the cathedral in the Valley. In the old days it was important in the lives of the people . Animals grazed on it. And it was a rich provider of peat. Browne-Willis in his *Survey of the Cathedral Church* said that the peat of Dowrog was peat of a poorer sort that came from a common which, in his estimation, was three miles long and 'came up to the town's end'. Poor it may have been, but it was conveniently near. Farm labourers

Maendewi, alongside Drws Gobaith on Dowrog Moor.

living in tied cottages had as part of their wages-in-kind two cartloads of peat from Dowrog, delivered free. Beams of timber laid crosswise have been uncovered deep inside it. Farmers and crofters have looked over it across the centuries, have threaded it with pathways, have kept it under control by grazing their animals on it, have filched from it, as Gerald of Wales said they had always done, and have very earnestly guarded it against strangers, and maintained their rights over it. The old Parish Council round the turn of the century reacted quite harshly to any threatened encroachment. When there was talk of a projected railway coming into St David's from Mathry Road and crossing parts of the moor on its way they bluntly refused permission. The Courts of the Manor of Dewisland were also very severe in their condemnation of any intrusions on this common land, and of any neglect of its boundaries. They also took care of its watering-places. But Dowrog is much smaller now than it was. So is the lake in its middle. On it at one time were flat-bottomed boats used by the farmers to reach their land on the other side.

It is a favourite haunt of wild-fowl and of sportsmen, and of butterflies in their season, and of wild crocuses. A West Wales Wildlife Trust pamphlet has described it as a unique mosaic of vegetation, a wealth of insect life, full of bullet-shaped frog hoppers, and green bugs, and black and brassy ground beetles, and wasps and hover flies. It now is well watched and supervised, and protected as a wet heath and marshland of special scientific interest.

The greatest charm of Dowrog belongs to something else, to its sense of secrecy, to a subtle suggestion of mystery, and to the equally subtle suggestion that through the centuries it has been a sanctuary. The gift of the common to pilgrims may have meant that they were being given a piece of land that would give them protection by authority of a prince. At least one bishop of St David's promised pilgrims a similar protection. But one of the most subtle suggestions that Dowrog was a sanctuary springs from a story—which is not actually a story, only the beginnings of one—that has been repeated time and again, orally, in print and in manuscript. It is a story of escape from religious persecution. It begins with the battle of Sedgemoor, 1685, where the forces of Charles II defeated those of the duke of Monmouth. Persecution under Judge Jeffreys and the Bloody

Assizes followed. Monmouth's followers had to flee for their lives. One group that escaped was a family of Dissenters in Bristol, who came to Pembrokeshire, were refused entry into Milford Haven and Porth Glais, and found sanctuary eventually on the moors of Dowrog. One of them was named Perkins.

The first register of members of Rhodiad chapel, a heavy tome, contains a history of the chapel from the beginning. A William Perkins of Pwllcaerog, a man who went to church but who had an open mind on religious matters, heard the Reverend John Richards of Trefgarn Owen preach in Carnachenlwyd, and invited him to preach in Pwllcaerog. From that sprang the introduction of Congregationalism in the district, the establishment of Rhodiad chapel, and eventually the establishment of Ebenezer.

The only difficulty lies in dates. The battle of Sedgemoor was fought in 1685. It was 1782 when William Perkins first met the Reverend John Richards. Heading the family tree of the Pembrokeshire Perkinses is the name of John Perkins of Pwllcaerog, 1697-1763. He married Ann Meyler, one of the Meylers of Rhosycaerau, thus uniting two dissenting families that became distinguished in the history of Pembrokeshire.

Rhodiad y Brenin (Congregational) 19 January 1785 to 11 December 1994.

One explanation is obvious—that the Bristol family of Perkinses were a distant branch of the Pembrokeshire Perkinses.

In any case, the story is firmly embedded in the family tradition. That accepted, Dowrog Moor, the sanctuary, played its part in the introduction of Dissent into this part of Dewisland.

[Sadly at 3.30 p.m. on December 11, 1994, Rhodiad y Brenin was disestablished, its doors closed for the last time.]

Dissent

'Because I am a Welshman,' said Gerald of Wales (proud of the one-third Welsh blood in his veins), 'am I to be debarred from all preferment in Wales?'

Four hundred years later came John Penry. 'Shall we,' he asked, 'be in ignorance until we all learn English? Raise up preaching even in Welsh . . . But why can we not have preaching in our own tongue?'

The one was a man of Norman blood who hated the Anglo-Saxons, who wanted Wales, and St David's in particular, freed from the shackles of Canterbury. The other was a Welshman who yearned to see himself and his countrymen in a situation where they could worship God in freedom in their own churches and in their own language.

Gerald's dream was not fulfilled till 1922 and the full disestablishment of the Church in Wales.

John Penry wanted a country cleansed of ignorance and superstition, a cleaner priesthood that could preach in Welsh, and a Welsh Bible. One reply to Penry's plea came in 1588 when the William Morgan translation of the Bible was published. The others were answered in the westward movement of dissent, the religious revivals of the eighteenth century and later the spread of education in the nineteenth century, and in the political and national awareness that followed these movements.

John Penry was martyred in 1593. Over a hundred years later an archdeacon of Carmarthen, Erasmus Saunders, wrote *The State of the Diocese* (1721) which roundly declared that the people were uneducated because the church had forgotten to teach them; that the church buildings were neglected, and become the solitary habitations of owls and jackdaws; that the priests were careless and given to absenteeism; and that they were poorly paid, and unable to preach and minister the sacraments because their training had been in English.

There were other reasons for this spiritual and material poverty. From the beginning of the sixteenth century down to 1874 there was no Welsh bishop, and no leadership. And by the eighteenth century 250 out of the 300 livings in the diocese had been taken over by lay people and country squires.

The consequences?

Archdeacon Tenison visited Llanrhian in 1710. He found that the vicar lived in St David's and very seldom visited the parish. Prayers were read once a Sunday at very irregular intervals, and the parishioners heard a sermon about once a quarter. There was a language difficulty: those prayers were read by an Englishman who was not understood in the parish. The result was 'that the people being disappointed of hearing prayers read in their own church in a language they are unacquainted with, go to hear an Anabaptist preacher in Llangloffan.'

Four parish churches, Mathry, Llanrhian, Llanhywel and Whitchurch, were on the parish boundary, but St David's is a large parish with the cathedral acting as parish church. There was nothing in between. It was a Master of the Cathedral Grammar School, Nathaniel Davies (1840-54) who told his dean of this remoteness.

> I am no favourer of Dissent, yet I keep coming to the conclusion that we are under infinite obligations to Dissenters for keeping alive a sense of religion in the minds of men, especially in places like St David's where from the extent of the parish it is physically impossible for the inhabitants to attend their parish church. Had two or three Chapels of Ease been erected fifty years ago and pious men appointed with sufficient incomes to minister to their pulpits and go about among the people during the week as diligent pastors of their flock, Dissent would be almost unknown at the present day in the parish of St David's.

It was too late. The dissenters were already there.

The problems of the parish were also problems of the diocese. There was a time when this diocese, part of the see of Canterbury, covered all of South Wales and part of Monmouth on to the borders of Herefordshire and Shropshire, a vast area of 1,275,000 acres. Dissent had to move across this vast block of Anglicanism. It came into Wales from across the border, and, drawing its strength from early Puritanism, it came in a determined mood. And waiting for it on the border were men who were prepared to lead, William Wroth and Walter Cradock.

It was William Laud, bishop of St David's from 1621 to 1627, who in 1662 issued a set of orders that were intended to regulate and control the services of the church: the second Act of Uniformity compelled obedience from all ministers. Those who refused were the first Dissenters, Wroth and Cradock and William Erbury. William Wroth was vicar of Llanfaches in Monmouthshire, Erbury and Cradock in St Mary's, Cardiff. Cradock was expelled from his curacy in 1633. In 1639 he came to Llanfaches, and it was there that he and Wroth organised a little gathering of secret worshippers into a new church, the first organised Nonconformist church in Wales, a mixed congregation, it is said, of early Baptists and Independents.

The Baptists were the first to come into Pembrokeshire. Their pioneering spirit was John Miles, an Englishman born on the other side of the border. He was educated in Oxford, joined a Strict Baptist gathering in London, and was sent by them to Wales. He established a church in Ilston on the Gower peninsula and worked closely with another church in Olchon in the district of his birth. From these two churches the Baptists spread westwards and eventually came to Rhydwilym, the mother church of the Pembrokeshire Baptists set on the border with Carmarthenshire. Rhydwilym was incorporated in 1668, its members coming from the three counties of Dyfed; and in its second year had 133 worshippers, 59 of whom came from 19 different parishes. Its second daughter church was Llangloffan.

It was trade, they say, that brought the Independents to Haverfordwest, religion following the trade routes, which was what Gwenallt meant when he sang of '*marsiandiaeth Calfari*' (the merchandise of Calvary). That trade almost certainly belonged to Bristol, on which Pembrokeshire and St David's were heavily dependent.

The early dissenters (and the Quakers, who left St David's in 1732) had to worship in secret and in fear. The tension broke when Peregrine Phillips, vicar of Llangwm and Freystrop, was dismissed after the 1662 Act of Uniformity, and began holding meetings of dissenters and lukewarm Anglicans in Haverford-west. That was the beginning of 'The Green Meeting' and Albany Church. Matters improved after 1689 when the Toler-ation Act allowed Nonconformists to worship in licenced houses. In 1724 the Independent chapel at Rhosycaerau was built, and in 1784 the first Independent chapel in Dewisland. This old chapel still stands dangerously ruinous and above its doorway is a message—

53

> This building was erected 11 June 1784, and opened as a place of worship 19 January 1785, and called 'The King's Way'.

That was the chapel of Rhodiad y Brenin on the coast road.

The distinction of being the oldest Nonconformist chapel on the peninsula belongs to Calvinistic Methodist Caerfarchell, on the very edge of the parish. Its first chapel was erected in 1763 and against strong opposition. It became noted for its Sunday School, and is the only 'first' chapel of which a ground plan exists. It was small, and plain, for those early Nonconformists disliked ornateness. They built their chapels like barns, and called them the granaries of God, *Ysguboriau Duw*. Many of their ministers were small farmers, sowing the Word of God as vigorously as they sowed their crops of oats and barley in their stony fields.

In the Magazine of the Historical Society of the Calvinistic Methodists is a little addition to the previously printed history of Caerfarchell chapel. On a page of the Bible of Elizabeth Evans of Solva (one of the *'plant yr eglwys'*, one of the children catechised by Thomas Charles of Bala when he visited Caerfarchell) had been drawn a plan of the ground floor of the original chapel which was erected in 1763 and pulled down in 1827. Here it is.

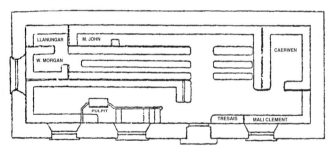

It took only thirteen days to build; but then it was only forty five feet by fifteen.

Those early days of dissent were days of fluctuation and of change. There was a time, obviously, when all citizens of a parish belonged, in theory at any rate, to the church. Some fell away through indifference or resentment. Some became attracted to the Baptists or the Independents; and some Baptists walked all those miles to Llangloffan or Middle Mill long before Seion in the city was built in 1842. The Calvinistic Methodists drifted from the church into their first gathering in 'The Black Lion' (behind the Lloyds Bank building of today) or chose to go to 'mother church' according to mood or conscience. They then began to meet in an upstairs room in Nun Street, then into their first chapel at the junction of Gospel Lane and New Street, then into the first chapel built on the site of today's Tabernacle, and then finally into the chapel of today that was erected in 1877. They were the last formally to leave the Church, for in 1811 they began to ordain their own ministers, the final break.

The dates that chapels carry are the dates of building. The adherents, the worshippers, were there much earlier, otherwise the chapels would never have been built. On the basis of these, Tabernacle was the first Nonconformist chapel in the city— 1785. Next came Ebenezer, 1818. On 20 November 1815 James Griffiths, minister of Rhodiad, had applied to Bishop Thomas Burgess for a licence to build, stating that he was satisfied that 'a certain meeting house called Ebenezer situate in a field commonly called Parcycycwyll (Quickwell Hill) is intended forthwith to be used as a place of religious worship by an assembly or congregation of protestants.'

Then, perhaps surprisingly, on 13 December 1824 another application was made in the name of John Roach announcing that a certain dwelling called Lleithyr was to be used as a place of worship. Yet this should not surprise us: before the time of chapels groups of worshippers, Baptist and Independent and Methodist, had been in the habit of meeting in cottages, for convenience or for fear, and in farms and in the open air. Many of the larger farms of the parish and around were in a very true sense centres of dissent, Pwllcaerog, Trefochlyd, Caerhys, Llaethty, Carnachenwen and Carnachenlwyd amongst them. Methodist Carnachenwen had regular Sunday meetings, and a Sunday School. There was a pulpit in the kitchen long before the pulpit in the chapel.

In May 1781 John Wesley came to St David's, probably on one of the forty journeys he made to Ireland. He disliked the place, saw the cathedral 'hastening to ruin', preached in the open air, and left a little gathering that had to meet in private houses for thirty-seven years until 1818, when against much opposition it built its first chapel in Goat Street. It is nowadays an English congregation. But at the opening services in 1818 three of the ministers who preached spoke in Welsh.

55

Berea Chapel—Sunday School trip to Goodwick, 1907.

Rehoboth. Induction Services of the Rev Dan Thomas, 1939.

56

In terms of chapel building the Baptists were the last to arrive in the city. They had their own distinctive way of organising things, with their mother and daughter churches, and their careful supervision: a daughter church had to prove its ability to stand on its own two feet before becoming fully recognised in the service of *'corffori'*. Llangloffan was established in 1745. In 1794 it released 70 members to form the church in Middle Mill (Y Felin Ganol). And Middle Mill in its turn released 99 members to form Seion in the city. Seion was formally recognised in 1866. Amazingly, it had taken the Baptists two hundred years to travel from Rhydwilym to the cathedral city.

In the little village of Tretio, a few miles out, stands another small Baptist chapel, now deserted and decrepid. It was built by a local farmer, Henry Bevan, and in its time served the local community, as its cemetery reveals. But it was built primarily because Henry Bevan's wife found herself no longer able to walk to Llangloffan. The Baptists were a determined people.

St David's is a parish of about 12,000 acres, and its population has never crossed 2,000, except in the middle decades of the nineteenth century. Yet it has been bespattered with churches and chapels and holy places and holy wells. The beginnings of its 1300 year Christian history were influenced by its geographical position; what came after sprang from the arrival of Dewi and the church he built.

There may have been a monastery here before his time. More than one church must have been built on the site of his monastery; one was dedicated in 1131, and pulled down to make way for Peter de Leia's cathedral. In the thirteenth century the Bishop's Palace was built, and St Mary's College in 1346. Then came the chapels of the coast built in times of medieval pilgrimage, commodiously seated, said Manby, to draw the devotion of the people. Capel y Pistyll (the chapel of the spring, near Porth Glais) was reputedly the chapel dedicated to St David. St Non's, built near the sacred well, was the chapel of his mother. St Justinian's chapel, restored by Henry Gower, commemorates the Saint of Ramsey. There was Capel y Gwrhyd on the coast road, and a chapel in the hospital at Whitwell (Ffynnonwen) established by Adam Beck in the thirteenth century. Some say there was a monastic settlement and therefore a chapel in Llandrudion. Caerforiog, the birthplace of

Adam Houghton, had its chapel. There were two chapels on Ramsey. In an adjoining parish was the chapel dedicated to St Elvis, Llaneilw. And on the dunes of Whitesands, marked now by a tablet, is the reputed site of a chapel dedicated to St Patrick.

That was how things were before the Nonconformist movements of the eighteenth and nineteenth centuries. Their continuing growth meant the building and the rebuilding of chapels.

Caerfarchell led the way, in 1763 and 1829. It was followed by Rhodiad (Congregational) 1784, 1849, 1893; Tabernacle (Presbyterian), 1785, 1827, 1877; Ebenezer (Congregational), 1815, 1838, 1871; Bethel (Methodist), 1828, 1877; Berea, 1833, 1878; Tretio, 1839, 1851, 1902; and Seion (Baptist), 1843, 1866 and 1897. Some had their little chapels of ease, little Sunday School centres in the outlying districts, Rhydygele, Treleddyd Fawr (Congregational and Methodist), Rhosson and Fachelych. And the smallest of them all, 'Y Twyn' or 'Slow Come Up', the little Baptist Sunday School cottage at the top of Whitesands Hill.

The nineteenth century also saw a resurgence in the life of the Anglican church, led by two eminent bishops, Thomas

Trelerw cottage church school, with thatched roof and bell turret. Closed c. 1916.

Burgess and Basil Jones, and by Dean James Allen. The cathedral church was restored. So was Whitchurch (the Tregrwes of the locals). In 1879 a new church, dedicated to St James of Compostella, was built at Carnhedryn. It was deconsecrated exactly a century later. In 1879 again St Aidan's Church in Solva was built; and a little Sunday School cottage, belfrey and all, was opened at Trelerw.

1300 years have passed since the time of David. His Celtic Church was a loose federation of churches, very different in organisation from the Church that came into eastern England from the continent and Rome, and very reluctant to fall into line with that Roman Church. There was dissent then, as there was in the churches of the New Testament. There always has been dissent. Our cathedral is itself a reflection of dissent. It was Catholic. When Henry VIII broke with Rome it became a cathedral of the Protestant Reformation Church. Today it belongs to the disestablished Church in Wales. The Catholics, who were here in Norman/English times, now have their church in New Street, dedicated to St Michael; and they have St Non's House, taken over by a Passionate Fathers in 1939, as a centre for pilgrimage and a retreat for all church people.

The dissent of Puritanism tried to break away from the Established Church, and led to what became the Nonconformist movements which were responsible for the chapels of today. These Nonconformist movements took a long time to reach the city, but they came. Today the cathedral is where it was from the beginning, in the Valley, parish church and centrepiece. Standing on the brink of the high ground around it are the four Nonconformist chapels. Between city and chapels and cathedral are the Thirty-nine Steps, reminiscent of the Thirty-nine Articles on which the Anglican Church was based.

Like the ebb and flow of the tide, all these and the religion they encompass have had and still have their influence on city and parish. Dewisland is steeped in religion, and strewn with churches and chapels and holy wells and places. And the legends of the Saints.

Plygain

The old farmers of this parish were immensely conservative, on their farms and in their chapels. They kept to a firm calendar of events, geared to the seasons of the year, and to their rituals. So did the chapels where they worshipped. Things are different now. Congregations are smaller; the chapel is no longer the centre of social life. There is, however, one chapel that for a hundred years and more has kept in its calendar a custom that is a Nonconformist adoption of a much older service of the parish church.

The time of day approaches six o'clock in the morning.
The day, Christmas.
The scene, The Square and Goat Street.

They come in their ones and twos and threes, some young, mostly old, male and female, bescarved and buttoned up, bleary eyed, unshaven some, their hail mornings bright and loud, the words of their mouths making spidery webs in a crisp morning air. One single lamp guides them down the slope and they have arrived—at the vestry of Tabernacle Presbyterian Church. Fifty perhaps, where once there was a hundred, Welsh, but with a steady addition of English, members of many churches in and around city and parish, all of one mind. Brightness is in the air, for this is *Plygain*, an old festival of Christmas day.

The word *plygain* is sometimes spelt *pylgain*, but the correct form is *pylgaint*, a word that comes from a combination of two Latin words, *pulli*, which means a young cockerel, and *cantus*, which means song. *Plygain* therefore means 'cock-crow', and by implication 'the return of light or the early morning or dawn' (as one old dictionary declares). The Old Romans divided their twenty-four hour day into quarters and *plygain* originally coincided with the third of these, between midnight and 3 a.m. Or rather it did, for the cockerels of the west woke later, and the *plygain* of the west came to mean between 3 a.m. and 6 o'clock. The first meaning of *plygain* then is the time of daybreak.

The word entered into the language and literature of the Welsh at an early age, and into the language and literature of the

60

church. We find *plygain* and *gosper* in *The Black Book of Carmarthen* (compiled in the late thirteenth century) and in the Book of Common Prayer in the sense of morning and evening prayers. And *plygain* as morning prayers (matins) appears in the works of William Salesbury, the sixteenth century translator of the New Testament into Welsh.

Tabernacle Presbyterian Chapel.

61

But the calendar of the church also shows that it was once linked with holy communion. In the *Sarum Missal* (the book of church services compiled in Salisbury in the eleventh century) were listed three masses, one for midnight and called Callicantu (which has the same meaning as *pullicantus*), a celebration of the birth of Christ, and two others, one to celebrate the bringing of good news (by the shepherds), the other to celebrate the eternal son-ship of the Holy Child.

In that way *plygain* became associated with midnight mass, and with Christmas. But not in Wales, where it became, in church and in chapel, predominantly a prayer meeting. The remarkable thing is that the celebration of *plygain*, whether in church or in Nonconformist chapel, was invariably a regional affair, dependent on the feelings or traditions of each particular area. And the content of the service, and its timing, also depended on what can be called regional taste. There was never any consistency.

Two characteristics of *plygain* emerged during the last century. First was the prominence of carols. These were long and complicated, sung to humdrum tunes, but remarkably comprehensive: they dealt with the essentials of the Christian faith, and with the history of Christ's life on earth. Some were so complicated and long that professional carol singers were engaged to sing them, and they were paid for their services. Sometimes these carols were sung to the accompaniment of the harp. Their influence on the congregation must have been very considerable, and they were popular, so much so that the *plygain* service was sometimes announced as 'a meeting for Christmas carol singing'.

The other characteristic concerned candles. *Plygain* was a celebration of the birth of Christ, the coming of the Light of the World. But chapel or church at six o'clock in the morning, or earlier, was in darkness, and illumination was required. Parishioners, worshippers, therefore, brought candles, sometimes of various colours and often decorated with paper wrappings. *Y Genhinen*, the quarterly magazine published between 1883 and 1928, printed an article on the practice.

> December 29, 1864. I was at a meeting at little Capel y Wig in Glamorgan. I was amazed to see a great number of candles—many scores—of all colours and sizes—placed to decorate the chapel. I was told that it was a very old custom.

The custom of placing lighted candles in chapels at Christmas was a very common practice in South Wales about the year 1864. Hardly a family of the congregation avoided preparing candles dressed in coloured strips, and bringing them to the *plygain* which was a prayer meeting held as early as five o'clock on Christmas morning.

A *plygain* service from the Calvinistic Methodist chapel of Mynydd-y-Garreg in Carmarthenshire was broadcast in 1946. A publicity note on the broadcast commented—

> An interesting old custom in conjunction with the service was that everyone who attended used to take a few candles so that the Chapel would be brilliantly lighted. What remained of the candles were then handed over to the caretaker immediately after the service and were used for lighting during the ensuing year.

It was, then, a service of colour, candles and carols. But that article in *Y Genhinen* also made the wry comment that the Christmas candles and the plygain service itself were relics of Papism in Wales.

The custom of carol singing eventually disappeared, to be replaced by the singing of Christmas hymns from the various denominational hymnbooks. *Llyfr Hymnau a Thonau y Methodistiaid Calfinaidd* of 1859, prefaced by Ieuan Gwyllt, makes no

Cross Square, from an old postcard, *c*. 1914.

reference to carols. An old and undated copy of the *English Congregational Hymnary* has fifteen carols. *Y Caniedydd Cynulleidfaol Newydd* of 1927 has three. And *Llyfr Hymnau y Methodistiaid Calfinaidd a Wesleaidd* of 1927 has three.

Evan Isaac, who was Wesleyan Methodist minister in Bethel, Goat Street, during the 1930s, and who wrote a book on old Welsh customs, *Coelion Cymru*, made this comment on *plygain* as practised among the Nonconformists—

> It was a religious service, held before daybreak on Christmas morning, to celebrate the coming of Jesus Christ on this earth. It was a service that had much singing and praying and thanksgiving, along with some kind of sermon or short address. When *Plygain* was at its most popular the singing of carols was an essential part, but I never heard a carol sung in *Plygain* or any other service. By the time I had reached my teens, there was hardly any difference between *Plygain* and an ordinary prayer meeting.

Tabernacle Presbyterian chapel is no more than a few hundred yards from Bethel, Evan Isaac's Wesleyan (Methodist) chapel. It remains a chapel that is strongly aware of its traditions, evangelical and Sankey and Moody in many ways. It has a fine organ, and a traditional love of community singing. And it still holds its *plygain* service at 6 o'clock on Christmas morning, the only chapel in the parish, perhaps the only chapel in south-west Wales, that still clings to *plygain*, and to a certain pattern of worship as part of its tradition.

In 1946 the *Caernarfon and Denbigh Herald* printed the following note on *plygain*—

> It is reported to be over a hundred years old and has been held without a break for many years. People used to attend the service which begins about six o'clock in the morning, and after a prayer has been offered, an impromptu programme of carols is rendered. There is no set programme, and those attending volunteer to sing, and by the time that they are out it is broad daylight.

In many respects that is not so different from the pattern that Tabernacle follows today. There are prayers and readings and singing, following a very short introductory address planned to cultivate an atmosphere of humility and thanksgiving, and then a time when worshippers can make their own contributions. The spirit perhaps is more important than anything else.

The feeling that one has tried to come, has made the effort, has conquered all kinds of inhibitions, indifference, discomfort, cold, to be there. Men and women, young and old, make their way home with a feeling of deep satisfaction that something has been aimed at and achieved.

Tabernacle has one other claim to distinction. It has its own carol, composed by the man who, from 1884 to 1920, was the first secretary of the chapel. 'Carol Nadolig' by David Evans is sung in St David's every Christmas season.

Street Names

The two main streets of St David's are High Street and Nun Street, running east and north from Cross Square. Looked at from the other direction, there are the two traditional land entrances into the city, meeting on the Square around which the city grew. Goat Street must also have been of some importance, leading as it does to Porth Glais.

High Street has never been anything else than High Street, right up to Grove Hotel. Nun Street, on the other hand, has grown and absorbed a number of extensions, Trehenlliw Terrace, Royal Terrace, and Oakley Street, which were infillings to accommodate the demand for houses. But why Nun Street?

Was it named after St Non, mother of our Patron Saint? According to old records, without question, yes. There is a will of a Richard Owen, proved in Carmarthen in 1606, whereby he gave to his sister some land 'situate in St Nunnes St.' Brown-Willis's *Survey of St David's Cathedral* (1715) mentions 'St Nun's St.' George W. Manby's *History of the Parish of St David's* (1801) also calls it Saint Nunn's Street, and this perhaps was the last time it was so recorded.

St David's mother, after the birth of her son, according to legend became a nun. The old chronicles used the word 'Saint' correctly. It was Richard Fenton who ignored it. His *Historical Tour through Pembrokeshire* (1810) tells that the city (apart from the Close) was regularly laid out and distributed into streets, lanes, and alleys, High-Street, New-Street, Ship-Street, Pitt-Street—and Nun-Street. By omitting the word 'Saint' he broke the connection with David's mother, and allowed another interpretation to emerge, linked with the common noun 'nun'.

Was there ever a nunnery in Nun Street? A lease of 1853 mentions 'a vault and old buildings and garden in Nun St.' This according to the *Tŵr-y-Felin Guide* (1915 and 1923) was known to the old people as 'Yr Hen Fowt' (the old vault) and stood at the corner of Gospel Lane and New Street. The bottom storey was stone-vaulted, and had but one four-paned window facing the street. The Tithe Commission Map and Schedule of 1838, signed and sealed by the Commissioners in 1842, states that Number 94 in Nun Street was part of an old nunnery. The *Tŵr-*

y-Felin Guide again says that a few traces of the vaulting of this old structure could still be seen in 1923. Beyond that there is no definite proof that there was a nunnery here.

Quickwell, road and well, has a very different story. A glance at the O.S. Map shows that the parish is full of springs. The old farms had three in some cases, within reach of the kitchen door. So have many of the city's better houses. There are scores of springs alongside Goat Street and the road to Porth Glais.

Rhygyfarch's *Life of St David* tells the stories of at least six sacred wells that were so important in Celtic life and religion, both pagan and Christian. Some of these wells are now dried up. Some are no longer identifiable, like Ffynnon Dunod. Some, like Whitwell, where Bishop Adam Beck established a hospital and sanctuary for the sick and old, have been sealed. But Quickwell is still alive and working, protected and restored. And it has three histories and three names.

No Saint's name was ever attached to Quickwell. In that sense it is not a sacred well. On the flyleaf of a seventeenth century volume of *Liber Communis*, the cathedral account book, a scribe asked the question: 'Breghys well—ubi?' He knew the name, but he didn't know where it was. It was then known as a burghers' well that belonged to the burghers, the burgesses of the borough, as St David's was known in Norman times. It was a public well. The minutes of the first forty years of the Parish Council, post 1894, reveal the anxiety of councillors over the public water supply: wells demanded constant cleaning and deepening. Not so long ago the debris at the bottom of Quickwell was cleared out and a trimmed rectangular stone was uncovered on which were the words—'This well was repaired by subscription AD 1813.' This was a citizens' well.

It has also been known by a Welsh name, Ffynnon Cwcwll. Wells meant fertility, life; they had to be protected against flooding and drying up. They were given guardians, a priesthood of the well. Near the holy well of St Non, they say, was once a house in which lived the guardian of the well. The Christians, of course, sanctified these wells and gave them the names of Saints and built little chapels alongside them. The Welsh name for the cowl, the headgear of a priest or monk, is *cochl*. The Irish name is *cochul*. And the other name for the monk's cowl, coming from the Latin, is *cwcwll*. Ffynnon Cwcwll, then, is a well with an arched covering or a hood that looks like a cowl.

Goat Street today (or Ship or Sheep or Pit Street).

Old cottages that once were on the Penlan side of Merrivale, *c*. 1895.

This well bears the same name as the road on which it stands. That road goes downhill and arches its way towards Penitence Bridge and Boning's Gate. But there is another way down to the Close, down the steps to Bonws Lane and alongside a field called Parc y Bonws. 'Bonws' is a corruption of the English word 'bone-house', a charnel house. The waters of Quickwell are said to have once fed the Cathedral Close (as the waters of Whitwell are said to have once fed the Deanery) and passed through the crypt under St Mary's Hall. That, they say, was once a charnel house. Is Quickwell then an echo of the words of the Prayer Book—'the quick and the dead'?

High Street, like Nun Street, has undergone a process of filling up. When Basil Jones (later bishop) and E. A. Freeman (the two great scholars who wrote *The History and Antiquities of St David's*, 1856) saw High Street as it was, they saw a gentle declivity, consisting chiefly of mean houses, a few of them thatched, and all of course whitewashed, and built so irregularly as scarcely to deserve the appellation of a street.' A gap-toothed string of courtyards, gardens, pigsties, and mean houses.

Goat Street? Nobody, not even the solicitor antiquarian of St David's, Francis Green, ever tried to explain the 'Goat' element. It has also been known as Ship and Sheep Street. Ship, understandably because it is on the road to Porth Glais. 'Sheep' may well have been a gradual corruption of 'Ship'.

The Pebbles, the short one-sided street from the Square to Tower Gate, is sometimes called The Popples. One half of its width was at one time paved with pebbles, or cobbles or popples.

Back Lane, running parallel with High Street, is now rapidly filling in. In Eiluned Lewis's *The Captain's Wife* it was 'country . . . not forbidden country . . . but the beginning of all adventure.'

Gospel Lane had the first of the Calvinistic Methodist chapels at its junction with New Street, and possibly that mysterious nunnery at the other end.

Mitre Lane once had a pub of that name.

New Street until not so long ago was just that—the beginning of further development towards the north.

The mystery street, the lost street, is Pit Street. Francis Green's article, 'The Streets of St David's City' (in *West Wales Historical Records*, *Volume VIII*) simply states that Pit Street stretched from the Square down to Tower Gate. Hi didn't know that four years earlier the map that accompanied the sale brochure of the Trefacwn estate (1919) showed Pit Street at the bottom of Deanery Hill. He could not have known that the large scale Ordnance Survey map also has Pit Street at the bottom of Deanery Hill. He never had the chance to know that when Queen Elizabeth and the Duke of Edinburgh visited the cathedral in 1982 the official police notice on the royal route stated that they would leave the cathedral by the West Door and proceed towards St Patrick's Gate and then along Pit Street and Goat Street and up through the Square to Haverfordwest.

Where is the explanation?

The Pit must refer to the low ground of the Valley and the Close. Visitors to the city and the cathedral in the old days would walk down High Street, come to the Square which was then an open space, and see before them the entrances of two roads down to the cathedral. The way from the Square to the Valley through the Popples and Tower Gate is the one traditionally associated with the great and ceremonial occasions. The other is through Goat Street, once one of the busiest roads in the city because of its connection with Porth Glais, and therefore where one would expect to find many business premises. The Highway Rate Book of 1870 published a long list of these business premises with their names and addresses and the names of their occupants. Many were said to be in Pit Street, far too many ever to have fitted into the Popples. The conclusion is that Goat Street, known once as Ship Street and Sheep Street, was also at one time known as Pit Street.

There is one contradictory fact. One of the older and private houses in the Popples is accredited to Pit Street.

Schools

On the eastern fringe of the city is a fine Georgian house built at the beginning of the nineteenth century of stones taken from the ruined vicars' choral quarters in the Close. Its name then was Grove House. Alongside this house in 1842 was a building that housed the Cathedral Grammar School, its vicar choral Master, and its classical scholars. In 1867 the school, still in Grove House, had a new Master, Alfred John Morgan Green. In 1868 Grove House was bought by William Williams whose parents owned the Commercial Inn in High Street, and he converted it into the Grove, the commercial hotel that it has been ever since. The Grammar School had to leave, and by 1870, according to the Highway Rate Book, A. J. M. Green had moved to Penygarn, where he had built a new home for himself and his school. Penygarn is now the Warpool Court Hotel. And there, two Masters later, and a short break, the Cathedral Grammar School closed its doors. The time was the early 1890s.

The Taunton Report on Endowed Schools (1868) referred to this school. The Collegiate and Grammar School at St David's, it said, had not been mentioned in any previous Government inquiry, but had existed for a very long time as a school for chorister boys, earlier even than 1363. In 1365 Bishop Adam Houghton and John of Gaunt, Duke of Lancaster, founded St Mary's College with a master, seven chaplains and two choristers to assist in cathedral services and to improve the singing. The choir school, obviously, had not been a great success. Adam Houghton had already turned his attention to the training and housing of his choristers and had become profoundly disappointed with the singing of 'priests in the western parts of Wales'.

St Mary's College survived the dissolution of the monasteries but surrendered to Edward VI in 1549. The cathedral choir was thrown back on its own resources. *Liber Communis*, the account book of the cathedral, recorded that in 1557 a new school building was put up at a cost of £10 15s. in the area west of the pathway between Deanery Gate and the cathedral south door. In 1564 an order was made that the young vicars choral

Cathedral Grammar School prize book label, in the time of A. J. M. Green (1867—1874).

CHAPTER SCHOOL
Sᵗ DAVID'S

FOUNDED A.D. 1363
BY
BP. ADAM HOUGHTON

and the choristers should attend school together, presumably in this new building. The order also listed some strict rules and punishments that suggested a previous lack of discipline. Vicars choral and choristers needed education and control.

That schoolroom of 1557 remained in use till the year 1791, when John Nash converted it into a Chapter-house. The school was then transferred to the old Chapter-house and Treasury, which are today's Cathedral Library.

The Taunton Report recognised the long history of this Grammar or Chapter School, seemingly accepting that it had developed from a former choir school. Jones and Freeman's *History and Antiquities* gives it one paragraph, and one reference in the index, and confirms that the room built in 1557 was the likely home of the school until the year 1791. But it also gives a wealth of footnotes to indicate that it was a very unsatisfactory school. Its standards in education and behaviour were depressingly low.

Francis Green of St David's was a meticulous researcher into cathedral records. He listed the names and dates of the vicar choral Masters and published the list in *West Wales Records*. There are thirty-six names on that list, beginning with Sir Harrie Jenkinson who in 1560 was paid 'for keeping the grammar school for one year'. With one exception (1874 to 1879) there is no break; everything suggests an unbroken succession, continuity. It was not so. The school that was moved to the old Treasury and Chapter-house in 1791 did not stay there. The facts lie in the Census returns. The 1841 Census proves that Nathaniel Davies, Master, was resident in Rock House (Y Fagwr) with a school of sixteen classical scholars. He had succeeded Jonah Owen, whose house it was, and who had been Master from 1829 to his death in 1839. In other words, the Cathedral Grammar School had left, or been thrown out of, the Cathedral Close. Nathaniel Davies carried on in Rock House for a while and then moved himself and family and school to Grove House. The 1851 Census proves that he was there with 21 scholars, some (boys and girls) from his own family, and others from Carmarthen, Taunton, Brighton, and two from Barbados. The school carried on in Grove House for some time under its new Master, A. J. M. Green and it was he who eventually, after the sale of Grove House, took the school to its last home, Penygarn, or Warpool Court.

Three men were involved in this change: Jonah Owen and Nathaniel Davies, Masters, and Llewelyn Lewellin, precentor in 1839 and then first dean of the cathedral in 1840. There could have been two good reasons for this change—the school's record was poor; and it must have been a financial burden. In addition, another chapter school had been established. The Benevolent School, established in 1812, was highly praised in contemporary reports; and the choirboys were sent to it.

In 1853, a year before leaving the Grammar School, Nathaniel Davies waged a fierce pamphlet war with the new dean. He accused Llewelyn Lewellin of having deprived the choir school of the endowments given it by Adam Houghton and John Morgan, bishops. The dean accused Nathaniel Davies of having made the Cathedral Grammar School into a commercial venture. The Master then accused the dean of neglect—when he came to take up his post he found that there was no schoolroom, no pupils, and no accommodation for himself. The dean replied by accusing the Master of having turned the School into a 'pocket Eton' classical fee-paying school, whose pupils were the sons of the gentry who were being prepared for the universities and the professions. In other words, the old Cathedral Grammar or Choir School had ceased to be; in its place a new type of school had been created (a fashionable type, because there were others in Solva and in Fishguard), that carried on under the old title, was still in charge of vicar choral Masters, and was still visited by the Chapter.

The Taunton Report came fifteen years after the pamphlet war. Green was the Master. The Report said that the choir school's considerable property, its endowment richness, was in the hands of the Ecclesiastical Commissioners. It had asked for assistance and had been given a very chilling response. And its curriculum? It taught Classics, Mathematics, Divinity and English, with Welsh 'if not objected to' and 'Navigation if desired'. It carried on for another twenty years and more, and died 'a natural death'.

That Report attributed its decline to the arrival of the railway in Haverfordwest, which enabled the gentry to send their sons to more distant and better known schools. There must have been another and stronger reason. State primary education had been established long before the 1890s. It was inevitable that state secondary education would follow.

In 1846 a commission was appointed by Parliament to inquire into the state of education in Wales. The result was the damning condemnation of 'The Blue Books'. The 1870 Education Act was passed and every parish had to submit a report on the state of education within its boundary. Samuel Williams wrote his report on St David's. His address to a meeting he chaired was sent for publication to *The Dewisland and Kemes Guardian* in which it appeared as a supplement on 21 January 1871, its aim being to prevent any misunderstandings. Samuel Williams quoted government statistics for 1846/47: the parish had 2363 inhabitants, 7 day schools and 253 registered students, and 10 Sunday Schools. By 1870/71 the number of schools had decreased from 7 to 6 and students from 253 to 236. He estimated that there were 400 children in the parish from 3 to 13 years of age, which meant, even allowing a wide margin, that there were at least 150 who were receiving no education at all. On the basis of these figures Samuel Williams made his recommendations, and the result was the establishment of the Board School in 1871, to accommodate 245 pupils, and the Church or National School, built in 1873, to accommodate 150 pupils. Both were built at the top of Quickwell Hill, facing one another across the road, and they are the schools of today, except that the Church School has moved to new premises in Nun Street that were officially opened in February 1969.

The 1870 Act established a general system of elementary education. In 1876 that education was made compulsory up to the age of fourteen; in 1891 it was made free. Secondary education had to follow. The Welsh Intermediate Education Act became law in 1889. In February of 1891 a Joint Education Committee for Intermediate Education in Pembrokeshire met in Haverfordwest. In June 1891 a public meeting was held in the Old Town Hall 'for the purpose of taking steps for an Intermediate School for St David's.' Certain conditions had been laid down by the County Committee: the locality had to provide suitable accommodation, including playground, for no less than 40 pupils, and for no less than five years; the school should be mixed; and there was to be a £5 capitation assessment, to accumulate at compound interest until the expiry of the five years. These conditions were accepted. Very soon afterwards the Old Town Hall was made available, Lewis Williams was appointed Head, and the school opened on 29 April 1895 with twenty-five pupils on the books. Lewis Williams did not stay long, and then Thomas Thomas of Brynberian Mills was appointed, and he stayed for thirty-two years. It was this man, like Owen Gledhill in Fishguard, who set the school on a firm foundation.

In May 1899 the Pembrokeshire County Governing Body informed the Charity Commissioners that the County Schools of Fishguard and St David's were to be put on a permanent basis. In July of that same year the St David's School Governors met to discuss plans and specifications for a new school. In September 1902 that new school was opened by Principal Griffiths of University College, Cardiff. At the official opening it was revealed that the total cost had been £1,800, of which £450 had come from the Governing Body and £500 from local contributors. Dean Howell was chairman of the responsible committee; Captain Roach was Vice-Chairman; J. Howard Griffiths, Priskilly, Treasurer; and W. D. Williams, Gwalia was first Clerk to the Governors.

One result of the Welsh Intermediate Education Act was entirely unanticipated. The general intention had been to establish smaller schools to teach a limited curriculum and one large school to teach the complete range. Instead, a large number of smaller schools sprang up in rural and small town areas, and they proceeded to expand their curriculum and teaching to the utmost. The Committee had never anticipated meeting strong local feelings and determined headmasters and dedicated staff. In his last term in school Thomas Thomas had three assistants and one part-time staff. He was then teaching 32 out of 37 weekly periods and was responsible for Latin, Mathematics and History. The initial salary for this post was £120 per annum, with an addition of £1 capitation for each pupil.

St David's Grammar School, now known as Ysgol Dewi Sant, celebrates its centenary in 1995. Its badge is the reverse of the cathedral's coat of arms, a black cross on a gold background, with five cinquefoils, presumably representative of the five-petalled rose of St David that flowers on our coastal paths in late spring. And the colours? They are the colours of Rhys ap Tewdwr, patron prince of the cathedral.

It could never have been a smooth road, from monastery to cathedral, to the choir school and St Mary's College and the Cathedral Grammar School, to state education, two primary schools set on either side of Quickwell Hill, and to a secondary school in a thinly populated but historic parish.

On that road there had been other schools. The Lingen (Blue Books) Report listed the Benevolent (established 1812), the Bethania Day School (belonging to Beynon's Charity, one of many in the parish), Ebenezer Day School (1842) and Tabernacle (1845), schools established by the Nonconformist chapels but not restrictive in their membership.

Samuel Williams's Report mentioned the Benevolent, and Miss Edmund's School, and Miss Appleby's in Royal Terrace.

There was a very popular church school held in a schoolroom in the Treasury enclosure, a building that was demolished in 1975.

76

The old school building (Y Bont) by Penitence Bridge.

And there was Dr Propert's School. William Peregrine Propert, barrister-at-law, lived successively in Prospect House and Cross House (Menai) and Manor House, and took his school around with him. He was vicar choral organist of the cathedral from 1851 to 1874.

Most of these schools had some link with the cathedral. Significantly, when state education emerged and the vicars choral departed, the big houses that they and their schools had occupied became private houses once again or developed into guest houses and hotels. Commercially St David's was becoming prosperous.

Squints

A squint is a narrow slit cut in the masonry of a church that allowed people from outside to catch a glimpse of the service of sacrament. Many old churches had squints. Llanwnda, dedicated to St Gwyndaf, is an ancient church on the Fishguard coast, once in the care of Gerald of Wales. It has a squint. So has Llanhowel church, probably built on the site of an ancient Celtic community.

But a squint can have another meaning: to peep, to look obliquely, to catch an unexpected view, to see something afresh. The artist gifted with a seeing eye and the portraying hand can commit to paper the odd glimpse of an old cottage, a broken arch in a ruin, the corner of a sun-trapped street. Graham Sutherland came to Pembrokeshire in 1934, and started painting St David's, and wrote of his experiences in 'Welsh Sketch Book' (*Horizon*, Volume 28). He saw them and wrote of them and must have drawn them, and here are the striking images for him—glimpses of a rocky path plunging down a mountainside, a fallen cromlech, farms 'glistening white, pink, and blue-grey', an inn crouching under low cliffs, the sun hinged on the top of trees, a horse's skull lying bleached on the sand, and the black-green ribs of half-buried wrecks.

There is no competition here with the broad and panoramic views—from the top of Carn Llidi; the white and flatter view from the bowl of Clegyr Boia, not so different now perhaps from what its earliest occupiers saw; and the unsurpassable view of the Close, cathedral and Palace and archdeacons' houses, and the river and the trees, that suddenly appears from the steps below Tower Gate.

These squints are glimpses, narrow angle views, catches of sea and island, glimpses of the upper stage of the Tower seen across the moor from Tretio, the humps of Ramsey looming unexpectedly from miles away; or the spire of Tabernacle caught as one comes down High Street, a sight that has been known to make goggle-eyed visitors think they were catching their first glimpse of the cathedral.

As good as any is the framed view from half-way between the cathedral's north door and St Mary's Hall: Llechlafar, the bridge of the talking stone between Domus juxta Pontem (once vicar choral property) and St Nicholas Penffos, a prebendal house once maintained from the revenues of Mynydd Du. Framed between these is the cobbled pathway up to the entrance to the Palace, on its right the high Treasury wall crowned at one time with masses of valerian. Here at one time walked white-habited Cistercians, monks from Whitland, and Dominicans, Black Friars from the priory in Haverfordwest, where William Barlow was prior. This was the road along which bishops and visiting dignitaries walked to the cathedral after the entertainments of the Palace. Then, a road of elevated pageantry. Today a sheltered grey-stone and cobbled lane.

Is there a squint in the cathedral? The sacred relics lie in a casket resting on a ledge within the wall of Holy Trinity Chapel. Through the grill that guards it, through a slit-window, you can peep through and see the High Altar and the Cross. Holy Trinity is, after all, the corridor along which in the great days of pilgrimage they walked their way from the south door to the north aisle and the shrine.

Writers and gossips and pilgrims often refer to the 'otherness' of St David's. One otherness, obviously, is the cathedral. Cathedrals were traditionally built to proclaim their universal message to the world. They were imposing, built to be seen. Our cathedral is hidden in a valley, built on a slope, its Close in a valley and straddling a little stream.

A very different otherness derives from the undulating nature of the countryside. The appearance of farmhouse and cottage can appear very differently when seen from different angles. Carn Llidi is a mere rock of 595 feet. From certain angles and in some weathers it becomes a mountain of impressive presence.

This changeability is linked with another otherness, which belongs to the light, the clarity that belongs to our unpolluted sea-washed air. Changes of weather and mists can have a remarkable influence on what we see, and those visions of islands around the coast have been explained as the influence of sunlight over mist.

It is a combination of these two, of undulations and air, that have made the peninsula remarkable from the artist's point of view. Graham Sutherland put it in words. It is, he said, 'magical and transforming . . . Watching from the gloom as the sun's

79

rays strike the further bank, one has the sensation of the after tranquillity of an explosion of light; or as if one had looked into the sun and had turned suddenly away.'

Is all this the secret of *hud a lledrith*, the magic and the mystery of this old and hallowed land?

The ecclesiastical squint provided the outsider with a view of a solemn ceremony inside the church. The squints of artist and photographer are glimpses of the unusual—Graham Sutherland's phantom roots or the twisted gorse on the edge of the cliff. There are squints of yet another kind that, although insignificant in themselves, may clarify our understanding of the past.

An entry of 1872 in the log book of the State Aided Primary School tells how Thomas James came and asked for his books. He had, while yet a mere child, to leave school and go to work in a coal pit. The economics of poverty.

Rachel Allen of Tenby came to visit her uncle, James Allen, second dean of the cathedral, when restoration was in full swing. She took a class in the Sunday School and, in an undated little essay, wrote of how she found 'it very funny to see the old people in school. There was one woman with a high hat on.'

No parish history can ignore the old news-sheets. *Dewisland and Kemes Guardian*, one penny every Saturday, was the area's first local paper. It had a curious beginning, arriving in Solva from London with three of its pages complete with national and international news. The blank page was then filled with local news and advertisements and printed in what is still known as Printing House in Lower Solva. The *DKG* later merged with the *West Wales Guardian* of Haverfordwest, and became notable for its articles on local history and for anonymous letters. In 1860 it reported that the Michaelmas Fair in St David's was declining, and that reaping machines had come to Pembrokeshire. In the same year, William Williams, mason, was charged with stealing apples from the garden of Mrs Mary Francis, and committed to prison for one calendar month. In January of 1875 the mail car from Haverfordwest to St David's carried the mails for the last time. And in 1876 a report from the St David's Farmers Club vouched that 'the cattle of St David's parish were good enough to stand against all comers'—a very strongly held local belief that grass and sea salts meant goodness.

The Alun stream past St Mary's College and running towards Llechlafar Bridge.

81

Squint at the Warpool orchard—where Jenkin D and Dewi R pinched apples
long ago.

In addition to local newspaper reports, there are other means, 'squints' that allow us to look into the life of the past, tales of 'the old chronicles', tales of age-old superstitions, family deeds, wills, family histories. A tale of bread in the next chapter reveals an old way of life and the beginnings of change. *Dyn hysbys*, the seer, has been a familiar and dreaded figure throughout history; here, a late survivor of medieval superstition. A document signed by master and tenant-craftsman is a social document of two hundred years ago. All these and a long 'squint' at the seven hundred year history of a farm combine to give us a brief history of this most conservative of agricultural communities. Here was *'crefft hynaf dynolryw'*, mankind's most ancient of crafts.

Bread

'I have not seen better or finer land,' said George Owen of Henllys, 'nor greater store of corn than I have seen growing about St David's.' The inhabitants of this land before his time and after lived simple lives. Their farms and smallholdings provided almost all they wanted. And corn was basic.

There was a time when the bishop, as lord of the manor, owned all the mills that ground the corn. This gave him a measure of control over his people, and some profit. Chaucer's Miller, we remember, loved the colour of corn, which is the colour of gold. He tested the quality of the ground corn, the grain, with his thumb, and he charged for his work, and the colour of his thumb was gold.

In later years resentment grew against this episcopal compulsion, and the people began in secret to use the quern, the small stone handmill. In later years people began to build small mills wherever there was falling water—at Lower Mill on the Alun (the bishop's mill); and at Pwllcaerog, Abercastell, Llanrhian, Caerbwdi and Middle Mill. Some of these old mills have now been converted into dwelling houses; some lie in ruins like the one on the sea edge, celebrated in Crwys's great Welsh poem, 'Melin Trefin'.

Melin Caerbwdi c. 1900.

The old Abercastell mill *c*. 1907.

Barley was the greatest crop ('especially barley,' said George Owen). Ground locally it was stored in bins for winter use in more forms than one. Edward Perkins of Pwllcaerog, who died in 1918, described the bread of his time. Some of it was *bara haidd*, which was barley bread, some *bara rhyg*, which was rye bread, the bread that made bone and muscle. Both were dark in texture, and tough. White bread was scarce and expensive.

Trepuet is one of the smaller farms on the eastern fringe of St David's, its owner at the end of the last century a shopkeeper in the city. On each of the six working days of the week his servants sat at the scrubbed bare board table in the *cegin fach*, the outer kitchen, to have their meals, dark brown bread and whatever else there was. Sunday was different; then there was white bread on the table. With them would be Shemi (James), head male servant living in, and as head servant in charge of the horses.

There came a Sunday when there was no white bread on the table. Shemi finished his meal, and went out and harnessed his horses, and went off to plough the fields. Sunday was not Sunday when there was no white bread. Ever since then Shemi was known as Shemi Bara Gwyn, James of the White Bread. The story is apocryphal, told of other farms and ploughmen. But there is general agreement that the early years of this century were the years of change.

The farmer folk and their wives had other uses for their dark brown flour. *Bwdram* was thin flummery, quite different from *uwd*, which was thick and served with milk. *Sopas* again was different. It consisted of uncooked oatmeal served with buttermilk, and was known as the best of all foods for the development of a paunch. Edward Perkins knew all of these, and, given a good harvest, he also knew that there would be enough brown flour, stored in scrupulously clean bins, to give him and his family a good winter's feeding—*bwdram* and *sopas* and *uwd*, and plenty of bread.

The standard baking day, incidentally, was Friday.

Trepuet and Pwllcaerog were comfortable farms. There were other and poorer places. One is described by Eiluned Lewis in *The Captain's Wife*. It belonged to the fringes of Dowrog, and Dowrog was always that little different. Outside a little cottage were two girls baking bread. Slabs of red glowing peat were stacked around an upturned pot. Inside was the baking bread, *bara tân mattau*, peat fire bread.

Last Will and Testament

All wills are testaments of concern. Old wills are revelations of concern and character and circumstance. The man who wrote his will, often under the guidance of the priest, was always 'of perfect memory, thanks be to God', and conscious of his mortality. He had already commended his soul into the hands of Him who had made him, and hoped for mercy and acceptance. And at the end he made his little gift to the cathedral church of St David, or to some other church, and gave his few pence to the poor of his parish. All wills were, and are, serious. He who owned little was as serious as the man who owned much. The very poor owned nothing and wrote no wills.

Charles Pigot, in 1757, gave to his granddaughter his most treasured possessions, his musical instruments. In 1777 William Propert of Trevigan made over to his sister Martha 'my brass and iron pots—except the largest brass pan which I give to my late faithful servant Hannah David from Castle Morris.' Henry Harris, vicar choral, in 1698 gave to the children one shilling each, 'on demand'. They were his brother's children. Thomas Roach of 'Llyther' in 1780 gave to his brother maintenance for life—or £7 yearly. And John Perkins of Tresunny, husbandman, gave his bedclothes to his three daughters, and to his son Philip, lambs, 'and to be kept in school till he be 15'. Thomas Johnes of the parish of St David's must have glowed with pride when in 1616 he willed to Gilbert Johnes 'a browne ambling mare' and to Richard Johnes 'a little red ambling colt.' The Johnes brothers were presumably his cousins. To Mary Green, 'my bedfellow', he gave all his household stuff and 'all that is lying in Llanungar in John Johnes haggards and £10 in lieu of all the thirds in my land.' He also did something that was not so uncommon, he bequeathed what others owed him. To one of his nephews he gave 20s 'due from David Gwynne' and to another 9s, 'due from Lewis Philip in the parish of Mathry'.

Thomas Martin of Gwrhyd Bach, who wrote his will in December 1694, gave to his grandchild Thomas John 'one fourth of my boat in Porthstinan harbour and all my hearing [herring] nets, he to pay the balance of my unpaid share in the same.'

Doorway into the kitchen, Gwrhyd Bach.

His is one of the most interesting of these old wills. He farmed land that was famous for its barley, barley that had to be harvested with care, that same care with which the Nonconformists harvested souls into their chapels, 'the barns of God'. He wrote almost all his will in terms of barley.

> To my youngest daughter Margaret David, widow, and her children, 3 bushels of barley out of the thirds that is in Trefelyn.
> To my grandchild, Elizabeth Rice, wife of James Rice, barley.
> To my son-in-law, David John, the residue of the barley at Trevely.
> To my grandchild, David John, barley.
> To the rest of my grandchildren the sons and daughters of David John, Gwrhydbach, barley.
> To my wife Joan Martin alias Miler, barley and sheep.
> To my kinsman Marmaduke Lloyd half a bushel of barley.

This parish drew its riches almost entirely from the produce of its land. Land that was good was scarce and valuable. Barley from that land was wealth.

Animals too were wealth. John Blethyne of St David's (one of the Elizabethan family that gave its name to Treleddyn) wrote his will in November 1682. This is what he wrote—

> To my daughter Alice a cow.
> To my daughter Elizabeth a heifer.
> To my son David stock.
> To my son Thomas a heifer.
> To my daughter Margaret a colt.
> The residue to my wife Elinor and my son William Blethine, they to be executors.

Probate was granted on 5 December 1682, and the inventory dated 22 November 1682 showed a value of £15 8s.

One of these old wills, each eloquent of private thoughts and possessions and kith and kin, is very different. It was the will of Catherine Williams, written in 1704. Here are parts of it—

> To my nephew Thomas Williams of Comodig the eldest son of my brother Thomas Williams of Carvoriog deceased 10s.
> To my niece Catherine Williams one silver spoon.
> To my sister Elizabeth the wife of David Harries of Treginnis Isha, a cow and 10s.
> To my nephew David Harries 40s and a colt.

To my cozen John Harris 20s and all my sheep with Edward Arnold in Porthmawr.
To my cozen Mary Harris daugher of Thomas Harris aforesaid 5s and two lambs.

Compared with those others, Catherine Williams's inventory is from another world. It lists one small silver salt cellar; 10 pewter dishes, 6 pewter plates, 12 pewter spoons; 2½ dozen wooden dishes, 2½ dozen trenchers, 2 brass candlesticks, and 2 cawks ('cawk', one assumes, is an anglicised form of *cawg*, which is the Welsh for bowl.)

This will was proved on 18 August 1704. The total value was £46.12.10. It included one item very rarely mentioned in these local wills and inventories. Catherine Williams had books valued at 4s 6d.

Hers, however, was not the only will to mention books. The inventory of goods of Thomas Perkins of Trevacoon made reference to two English Bibles, one Welsh Bible, and other small books.

One interesting reference is in the will of Henry Thomas of Trefochlyd Ucha, dated December 1686. He asked to be buried in Llanhowel Church, and followed this request with a remark-

Llanhowel Church.

able sentence—'I give towards buying a new Welsh Bible for Llanhowel Church, twenty shillings.' The Salesbury translations were made in 1551. The Richard Davies and Thomas Huett Bible should have been in every church in Wales by St David's Day 1566. William Morgan's complete translation came in 1588. What had happened to the Welsh Bible in Llanhowel? Or the Bible that should have been placed there? We shall never know.

Horse Talk

Edwin Pencarnan was ploughing Parc yr Odyn, the kiln field. The sea was all around him, and he was ploughing not with a tractor but with a pair of horses. In line with his nose was a single plough, and ahead his two horses, Bess and Dolly, and the single straight line of the last furrow but one. He had been there since early morning and would be there till the fading of the light, hoping to plough his one good acre in the day. And he had been there alone, his only companions his two good horses and the seagulls. And to break his loneliness he would talk to his horses, in the Welsh which was the language of his birth. Funny, though, that his horses carried English names and that his commands to them were in English.

Across the Sound, on Ramsey Island, Ivor Arnold was spending a year alone. His only companions were his two horses, some cattle and sheep, and the rabbits and the rats. The year was 1907. And every now and then, in those quieter moments, those strange bits of silence on an island, he would hear Edwin Phillips, talking to his horses, across a mile or so of Sound.

Traditionally and throughout the centuries the horse had been a privileged animal, the property of hunter and warrior, the aristocrat and the privileged, a prized animal in old Welsh wills—and the mount of the itinerant preachers of the Methodist Revival. It was once unthinkable that the horse should be subjected to ploughing, the most difficult of all labours on the farm. 'Neither horses, mares nor cows are to be put to the plough,' said the Welsh Laws. That was the work of oxen.

Then, sometime in the nineteenth century, and rather later in St David's, the horse became a working animal and was put to the plough. At the same time it became the most valuable animal on the farm, the prize of *mishtir* and *gwas mawr*, which is why it became the practice to site the stable as near as possible to the farmhouse. The horse became the most cared for, the best groomed, the best fed animal on the farm, and the best indicator of *mishtir*'s standing as farmer. That was how things remained until the 1930s, with the stables a blaze of colour—the blue and green and red and gold of the rosettes,

The now closed Agricultural Museum at Lleithyr. The 'double Tom' ridging plough and early track trailer plough.

prizes in the local show. From the 1870s onwards, naturally, ploughing matches became popular: in the White House (Tŷ-gwyn) and in Trearched in 1873; and in Trewellwell in 1876.

Fairs, however, from 1860 onwards, were in decline.

Agricultural change came slowly into this conservative parish. The Census Report of 1871 noted that 'machinery was being introduced with a consequent lessening of demand for manual labour.' Reaping machines came into the county in the 1860s. In 1874 there was a county trial of Hornby's reaping machines. And in the same year a local farmer advertised that he was prepared to cut anybody's hay (with machinery) at 2s 3d per acre. Tractors were slow in appearing; farmers continued to use horses for ploughing (possibly because of the stony soil) although a tractor of a later generation could in a day plough ten times what a pair of horses could do. Generally the farms of Cylch Mawr and Cylch Bach were the first to take in tractors; the stony soil lay in Cylch Gwaelod y Wlad. The little Ferguson tractor appeared in the mid 1940s. Ten years later the tractor was everywhere.

Yesterday's reaping (unidentified photographs).

And with the tractor came the impersonality of modern farming. A farmer talked to his horses. They knew him and his voice. That was the enormously affectionate bond between man and animal. No farmer loves his tractor as he loved his horse.

There are no working horses in the parish any more, no horses at all except in the riding schools. A few mounting blocks remain. The stables in the Close and in Grove Hotel—they too are gone, and with them the bridles and the saddles, the harness, the *mwnci* (which was the horse collar) and the bellybands. They were, so they say, thrown away to rot in the dark corners of outbuildings. The brasses—some of them were kept. They can still be seen, polished, in cottages and in the kitchens of farmhouses. And in the shops—on sale as souvenirs.

Lower Treginnis

There is nothing more depressing than a deserted farm. The farm was traditionally the home of a family who for generations had worked its land and cared for its needs. It in return provided them with almost everything they wanted. To see it deserted, no humans, no animals, no barking dogs, its farmhouse and outbuildings empty, the windows blank like the eyes of the blind: that is dismal, an impoverishment of life.

In 1974 Lower Treginnis was up for sale, and when bought was turned over entirely to the early potato business, which meant a farm without animals, a farm without workers except seasonally, a farm whose purpose-built old buildings had lost their purpose. In 1984 it was for sale again and remained empty till it was bought by the National Trust. The Trust then leased it to Farms for City Children, the teacher-organised charity project begun in 1976 by Michael Morpurgo in Nethercott Farm in Devon. In July 1991 it was officially opened by the Princess Royal, the second farm in this venture of hope.

The aim of this project was and is to get children of our inner cities out of their grim background and give them a week in the country, to breathe fresh air, to get to know country life and learn to love it, and to do a modicum of the everyday work of the farmer.

Lower Treginnis is not what it was, but it is still a farm, stocked, and the land taken care of by the occupants of Upper Treginnis. Some of the old buildings remain true to their original purpose. The restored double farmhouse is occupied by the resident master and his assistant, and old outbuildings have been excellently converted to accommodate what the school requires. All in all, here is a retention of the old alongside conversion into the new, surrounded by a magnificent landscape. Across the Sound, barely a mile away, is Ramsey. To starboard are the Western Approaches and the Atlantic. Around the farm are two miles of coast, a headland of green grass and grey rock, and heather and gorse, under a swiftly changing sky. Here are two hundred and thirty acres and thirty one fields, and a history stretching back to the time of the Iron Age Celts. On either side of this peninsula, Penmaenmelyn (the headland of

96

yellow stone), are two coastal forts, on the one side the great rock fort of Clegyr Boia, on the other Castell Heinif. The Celts who built these were also pioneers of agriculture, and it is likely that they were the men who first cleared the peninsula of whatever wildness there was and made it into farmland. They were Irish Celts. Treginnis? It means the home of Ginnis, and Ginnis is a familiar Irish name.

The first recorded mention of Lower Treginnis belongs to 1283. It was then a manor of the lord bishop. In 1587 John William Philip Robin was lord of the manor, probably leasing it from the bishop. In the seventeenth century appears the name of that tough old Elizabethan Welshman, Thomas Lloyd of Cilciffeth in the Gwaun Valley. When he died in 1615-16 he was in possession of a vast estate in forty-two parishes, and in that estate were Lower and Upper Treginnis. In 1697 the name of Henry Harries appears, of the same family that at various times occupied Trefacwn and Tregwynt and Cruglas, and this family and its in-laws were as tenants or occupiers connected with Lower Treginnis till 1850, when Samuel Williams of St David's bought it and installed a tenant. From then on, tenancies and ownerships became chequered and short-lived compared with the past. Some farmed it in the traditional manner. To others the farm offered prospects of riches from a copper mine opened in the 1820s.

The old house from a drawing, in the National Library of Wales, by Henry Harries, owner occupier. Dated 1808.

Dewi R's first working day at Lower Treginnis, 1929.

Potato picking, Lower Treginnis.

Thomas Llewellin, owner occupier and squire from 1856, was easily the most colourful in that long line of owners and tenants. A flamboyant character, he held a lease of Ramsey Island and farmed Lower Treginnis in style. The 1861 Census revealed him as Commissioner and farmer employing 17 labourers. With him were a common law wife and her son, a housekeeper, groom, housemaid, cook, dairymaid, and a bailiff who with his wife and two children lived in Porth-henllas. He is credited with having built the white-washed round dovecote in the yard (straddling one of the two springs on the site) and the magnificent fold or *ffald* at the rear of the farm outbuildings, a high walled and finely crafted enclosure within which is a full acre of land.

Thomas Llewellin brought colour and style and money into Lower Treginnis. Heading the family tree is a John Llewellin of Pembrokeshire who had three sons. John died unmarried. Richard went to Bristol before 1756, became a brewer, and bought the Holmwood estate; his wife was the daughter of John Williams of Trearched, Llanrhian. The third son was Thomas Llewellin of Olveston Court, Gloucester, who lived in a fortified manor house, owned 1500 acres of land and was lord of the manor four times over. This Thomas Llewellin had a son who died unmarried leaving his estate to his nephew. Richard Llewellin had four daughters and two sons. One of these, another Richard, was born at Westbury-on-Trym in 1802, bought Tregwynt Manor, and became Justice of the Peace, Deputy Lieutenant, and High Sheriff of Pembrokeshire in 1840. He was educated at Oxford, was a member of Lincoln's Inn, and died unmarried in 1871. His brother, Thomas Llewellin, was also born in Westbury-on-Trym, and lived in Tregwynt Manor before becoming owner-occupier of Lower Treginnis. He died there in 1865. The two brothers returned to the land of their fathers. They now lie side by side in Granston churchyard.

The farmhouse of today shows some external modification, but it is a sketch in the National Library of Wales and dated 1808 that shows the old Lower Treginnis as it was when Henry Harries lived in it. It looks a dark, heavy, solid building, and it has a number of lean-to additions, off-shuts as Peter Smith's *Houses of the Welsh Countryside* calls them. And there, in the middle of the kitchen roof is a heavy cone-shaped chimney. In other words, Lower Treginnis was once one of that group of architecturally distinctive houses of the parish, Clegyrfwya, Llaethty, Porth-mawr, Pwllcaerog, Rhosson-uchaf and Tref-aeddan, that Romilly Allen listed in the January 1902 edition of *Archaeologia Cambrensis*. These were important houses, homes of families of some substance, and Lower Treginnis was one of them.

For most of its time Lower Treginnis must have been worked on the traditionally conservative Welsh mixed farming style, well stocked, and as in the early years of this century growing hay, oats and barley and mangolds. In 1929, two brothers, James Harry and William Howard Thomas, tenants and later owners, added to that list. They planted as a small scale experiment a few drills of early potatoes, and sold the produce locally. That was the beginning of what was to become a vastly enlarged business in this area of the Gulf Stream, a business that could lead, and did, to large profits and equally large disasters.

The climate of this peninsula is good. Grass grows well, fertilised by the salts of the sea breezes. And the soil is quite extraordinary—it is very stony and these stones help to retain both heat and moisture. It is called 'trap land', and is deceptively rich, good for growing grass and for rearing cattle. Its deceptive nature is revealed in the story of 'the foreigner' (told in the *Journal of the Agricultural Society, Volume 23*) 'who arrived recently (1887) in the district, picked up the stones and carried them out of his field, for the sake of tidiness, and as his crop failed, he carried them back again, for the sake of fertility.'

The local farmer, of course, knows his land. It is, he says, full of *rwmbwls*. On Penmaenmelyn he won't set his plough to cut more than eight inches of a furrow, and in some parts no more than five inches.

Things change, and Lower Treginnis has seen more changes in the last ten years than for centuries. The coastline and the islands remain; the visiting children will see them but they will never see what the old farmers saw. They saw the slow-moving changes of the past; their descendants have seen the rapid immensity of modern change. And the story of Lower Treginnis is by and large the story of most farms of the parish throughout the years: a hard life, of plain and simple food and plenty of it; a life of religious thrift, careful of tomorrow, geared to the cycle of the years. And according to the reminiscences of the 'old

City Farm.
Farms for City Children project, Lower Treginnis, in 1994.

chronicles' a life that was happy within its limits. Edward
Perkins of Pwllcaerog called it living *'wrth ei ddeng ewin'*, a
man holding on with his ten fingernails.

It is said that these old farmers could read the face of the land
and the sea, and the sky, and could look through the face of the
stranger. Most of all they knew their land and the surrounding
sea. They had their boats and went fishing for mackerel in the
bay. The Lower Treginnis people, incidentally, had a landing
stage at Carnarwig. And from Carnawig—or from St Justinian
—eight hundred years ago a ferry ploughed its regular way to
Ramsey. It's all in *The Black Book of St David's*.

101

Social Contract 1792

That brief history of Lower Treginnis was in effect a peek at events in the life of one particular and important farm on the peninsula. The Social Contract of 1792 is another surreptitious glance—at a legal document incorporating the relations between a substantial farmer, a *mishtir* and his neighbour, who in effect was his craftsman tenant and helper. The details are in an indenture, which must have been one of two: the cuts and indentations on the upper edge of one had to match the cuts and indentations on the other; that was the meaning of 'indenture'.

The year is 1792. The farm, Tremynydd on the map, is known locally as Tremwni, and the farmer is Thomas Meyler, gentleman, member of an old and significant Pembrokeshire family, prominent in farming, very well known in the Congregational life of the county, and in its administrative life. The indenture was between this Thomas Meyler and William Jones of 'Gworyd', which was Gwrhyd, 'for the consideration of a yearly rent covenants provisos and agreements hereinafter mentioned.'

And the contents?

. . . to William Jones all that his present dwelling house and garden and also the free liberty to build or erect a convenient cottage to keep his cow adjoining the garden situate and being on part of the tenement of Tremonny aforesaid and which house and garden were lately built or erected at the expense of the said William Jones, together with one slang or stang of barley ground and one stang of ground to sow oats in yearly . . . the barley and oats to be sown yearly in such place or part of the said farm as to adjoin the corn of the said Thomas Meyler . . . Thomas Meyler doth promise and agree to cultivate the land for barley and oats with all proper and necessary tillage in a husbandlike manner and also to carry all the dung . . . and . . . yearly to manure the same . . . the said William Jones shall have free liberty to keep a cow on the tenement of Tremonny . . . with the cows of the said Thomas

[A slang or stang was a long strip of land, varying in size according to how the 'pole' was measured. And that could be from nine feet to twelve feet wide, according to the quality of the land. 8 poles × 20 would make a slang. So would 4 poles × 40. Matts were slabs of peat.]

Meyler . . . for and during the full end and term of ninety nine years . . . at the clear yearly rent of two pounds and five shillings lawful money of Great Britain.

. . . the said William Jones shall . . . well and sufficiently maintain and keep the said dwelling house, cowshed and garden hedge in good and sufficient repair.

. . . the said William Jones shall and will provide and send one able man to reap and bind constantly in the harvest yearly . . . at the rate or wages of four pence the day on the tenement of Tremonny aforesaid . . . the said William Jones shall and will work his trade or occupation of carpenter at the rate of six pence per day when and as often as he the said Thomas Meyler . . . shall have occasion or require it to be made during the time he shall be thought able and capable to perform the same on the tenement of Tremonny only.

. . . the said William Jones shall have free liberty to send two men for one day to beat matts on such part of the tenement of Tremonny as other tenants of the same place shall be permitted yearly . . .

. . . the said Thomas Meyler shall and will send carts to carry all such matts and also as much matts as two men shall beat out in one day at the common land called Dowrog . . .

. . . and also the carriage of one sufficient load of culm from the usual coal pits or any other place of the like distance yearly . . .

There is no evidence that St David's farmers of the eighteenth and nineteenth century were overfond of litigation. But, judging from the great numbers of indentures, large parchment documents, imposing, finely inscribed, that can be seen in some of the old farms, the scribes certainly were busy. Thomas Meyler in the following year of 1793 was to sign another agreement, with David Beynon of 'Tymunnus'.

But what did William Jones get out of his agreement?

He had a lease of 99 years on a house at Tremwni that he had built at his own expense and that he had to maintain. He had a garden whose hedge he must maintain—Gerald of Wales had said that the Welsh were fond of digging up boundary ditches, removing limits and transgressing landmarks. William Jones had the right to build an outhouse alongside his garden. He could keep a cow along with the Meyler herd, and had a slang of barley alongside the Tremwni barley and a slang of oats alongside the Tremwni oats. He had the right to get a day's cutting of peat from Tremwni, and a two man day's load of peat matts from Dowrog. He was assured of a load of culm, delivered. And

Ruins of Spite Cottage on Lower Moor. (Spite from the Welsh 'ysbaid', a moment of rest; or from 'hospitium', the pilgrim rest house).

Gwrhyd Bach, thatched and with slated eaves, c. 1895.

Thomas Meyler had promised and contracted to cultivate his tenant's slangs, and to carry dung to manure them.

What about Thomas Meyler? He gets a rent of £2 5s yearly (a lot of money in those days, the equivalent of 90 days' work at the carpenter's rate of pay). He gets one man's labour (an open-ended contract) for harvesting at 4d per day. He gets one carpenter's skilled labour (again an open-ended contract) for all repairs to be done at Tremwni at 6d per day. In fact, he gets a monopoly of William Jones's craftsmanship during all 'the time he shall be thought of able and capable to perform'. And he has the right, if William Jones defaults in any way, to walk in and possess the house and land, land that was already his.

Did it work? We do not know. Was it a variation on the system of tied cottages? Did William Jones tie his life and labour, his craftsman's skills, his cottage, in a way his life and family, to Thomas Meyler? The 99 year lease also suggests a desire for continuity, of son to follow father, as actually did happen often. The indenture tells us what the agreements were between one particular farmer and his craftsman labourer. The later history of the arrangement we do not know. Thomas Meyler, the man who signed the indenture, died in 1807.

Prophet of Doom

The green grass of this parish grows right up to the cathedral walls. And around cathedral and city is the circle of old farms, some of whose names can be found in the *Black Book*, the 1326 record of the bishop's lands. The families that lived in them for generations are now fast moving out, and with them an old Welsh way of life, its customs and language, and quite likely some of the secret explanations of old place-names. The farm names remain, some in oddish forms. Cornwall has its Pol- and Pen- and St David's its Pen- and Llan-, and both have Tre- and Tref-, ancient homes of family and tribe. And all these prefixes are seen to be linked with a feature of the landscape, or the hero of a legend, or most of all the name of a Celtic Saint.

According to the Mabinogion story of Culhwch and Olwen, King Arthur and his hosts landed in Porth Glais to continue their hunt for Twrch Trwyth, the prince who for his misdeeds had been changed into a boar. On the road to Whitesands or Porthmawr is a farm called Penarthur and on St David's Head is a collapsed cromlech called Coetan Arthur. Trefaeddan carries the name of an Irish Saint, Aeddan of the Monastery of Ferns, who went into voluntary exile and came to the monastery of David. He was also known as Maeddog, and in this form is commemorated in Ffynnon Faeddog, Maeddog's Well, near Porth Mawr. Was Madog of Trefadog another Saint? And who was Iago of Treiago? Or Eynon of Hendre Eynon? Or on a different level and now on Ramsey, who was Mrs Morgan of Ogof Mrs Morgan? Or Mary of Ogof Mary? Or the John Owen who gave his name to Trwyn Sion Owen?

Some other farm names are different and curious from another point of view. Off the coast road beyond Waunbeddau is a farm that on the OS map is named Tremynydd, the settlement of or on the mountain. But there is no mountain here, as there is no mountain near Mynydd Du on the same coastal road. The locals refer to Tremynydd as Tremwni, and the meaning becomes clear when we remember that there is an old Irish word *mwni*, meaning a grove or bushes on rough ground. The old farmers of St David's used to say that they were going out to work on the *mwni*. One of the names given to David's monastery, after all, was 'Chell Mwni', the monastery of the grove. The vernacular can often lead us to the correct explanation and meaning.

Skyfog, a mile or two east of the city, must be a mongrelisation or an anglicised form of 'Ysgeifiog'. Trellwyd, dissected, means 'the grey home'. The locals call it Treliwyd. Treleidir may have nothing to do with *lleidr*, thief, nor with the story of the lad who was found playing with pellets of gold on St David's Head.

In the same area to the north of the city is the farm called Trehysbys. The locals insist on calling it Trehysbwys. And it is this old pronunciation that takes us to an intriguing tale.

Traditional old Welsh country life knew what *dyn hysbys* meant. He was the old-time conjuror, magician, soothsayer, someone who knew more than his fellow-countrymen. He was, moreover, one who was oddly informed, who could look into the future and read what was to come. Was there a *gŵr hysbys* who at one time lived in this farm and left his name behind him? There was certainly a *dyn hysbys* not far away.

The time is the second half of the nineteenth century. At that time the Baptist chapel at Y Felin Ganol, not far from Solva, had a membership large enough to demand the pastoral care of two ministers. The senior of these, John Reynolds, was a local farmer and minister, a prominent man in the history of his denomination, and his home was at Treglemais. His assistant was a young man, William Jones.

Not far away from Y Felin Ganol is the village of Caerfarchell. That was the home of the soothsayer, William Howells, commonly known as Wil Tyryet, William of the house with the gate. It was this tailor who struck terror into the heart of a whole community and further afield when he prophesied the imminent death of William Jones, then a healthy young man. He aroused panic and terror, confusion, anger, and there were some who dared to mock his prophecy. His reaction was to make an additional prophecy—that at the funeral of William Jones there would be a stranger to the district, an unknown and elderly gentleman with a very long beard down to his navel.

In a few weeks William Jones was dead. A stunned people turned in morbid curiosity to the other half of the prophecy. The day of the funeral came, and the cortege started from the house and made its slow walking way to the chapel on the hill.

107

Caerfarchell Chapel (Presbyterian).

There was no white-bearded man in sight. The mourners arrived and entered the chapel, and there, sitting in the *cor mawr*, the big pew, was a man they didn't know. He had ridden across country, had arrived early, and had gone in to sit in the big pew to await the arrival. And he had a great white beard. He was no less than David Davies, first principal of Hill House Baptist College in Haverfordwest.

There were Cassandras in Greek and Roman legend whose prophecies were always prophecies of doom, and there were Biblical soothsayers, and prophets of the Old Testament, and nameless men and women in the Middle Ages, in England and in Wales, all prophets of trouble, natural disaster, human calamity.

There was one, a minor prophet, who lived in Caerfarchell. And another, perhaps, who lived in nearby Trehysbys.

Treleddyn

Francis Kilvert came to St David's in 1872, and was astonished by what he saw. Cottages and outbuildings (inside and out) were whitewashed all over. He was puzzled by this 'white country', 'kept on fancying that snow had fallen'. He was seeing Dafydd ap Gwilym's *'bythynnod gwyngalch Cymru'*. In the early years of this century Graham Sutherland came and painted these cottages in the 'luminous light' of this peninsula.

In 1840 the Tithe Schedule listed all the homes of the parish. There were some houses. Most were cottages, presumably single-storey homes. Then in the second half of the century came the building boom—the Old Town Hall was built by the Griffithses of Lleithyr; the elementary schools were built; and chapels built and rebuilt; and the cathedral restored. Thatch and zinc sheets were replaced by slates from Abereiddy and Porthgain. Later on these were grouted, and cottages were given their first floor. High on one pine-end of Treiago is a date-stone and on it 1880. Was it then that the single-storey cottage became a house?

That was how things were at the end of the last century and the beginning of this. There were, of course, those substantial farmhouses listed by Romilly Allen, eight in all, with two added later. He could have added Lower Treginnis, but didn't. Were there any 'big houses?'

Upper Treleddyn is without question a 'big house'. Its M shaped double-pile roof (a style that came into fashion in the seventeenth century, perhaps earlier) can be clearly seen south west from the top of the Pebbles. It sits on a breast of high ground, solid and square. Beneath it are two cellars where once the boom of the sea could be clearly heard; and legends once linked them with ghosts and smuggling and a tunnel all the way to Porth Seli. It was perhaps the only 'big house' outside the Close. In a dip in the ground below is a substantial farmhouse, Lower Treleddyn. And not far away at one time there was a cluster of five cottages known as Trenergy. It was, and looked like, an old settlement, manor house, farm, and labourers' cottages.

Treleddyn means the *Tre* or home of a family called Bleddyn, and there are documents to prove it. In 1529 a deed was drawn up between John Lunteley, Archdeacon of Cardigan and Master of St Mary's College and Richard Bleddyn of 'Treflethyn in the lordship of Pebidiauc', and in 1679 David Blethin of 'Trefflethin' gave a lease of the farm to Francis Laugharne of Llanunwas.

It was later, towards the end of the eighteenth century, that this fine house, this Upper Treleddyn, became attached to a legend of high and royal romance.

Benjamin Malkin called Haverfordwest 'the genteelest town in South Wales'. The county town drew itinerant players from Bristol (as we are told in Eric Freeman's *Historic Haverfordwest*), and famous London actors like Charles Macklin, and the Irish tragic actor, Theophilus John Potter, who came and stayed and made his name as printer and newspaperman. It was this dramatic activity, undoubtedly, that persuaded two daughters of a highly respected clergyman of distinguished ancestry to run away from home to the glamour of London's theatreland. There these two sisters, Grace and Mary Phillips, met David Garrick, and Grace met Francis Bland, disinherited son of a Dublin judge of a distinguished family whose origins lay in

The big house.

110

North Yorkshire. Four of the children of that liaison visited Treleddyn, and three, Nathaniel Bland and his sisters, Hester and Lucy, lived and died there. Their memorial stone stands in the south wall of the cathedral yard. Another, Dorothy Bland, joined her mother and aunt in a theatrical group that toured Ireland and the north of England. Her mother died in Edinburgh in 1789, her aunt earlier, in York in 1782. It was then that Dorothy Bland came to London. There she met Sir Richard Ford (whose father was one of the proprietors of the Drury Lane Theatre) and had three children by him. And it was at this Theatre Royal, Drury Lane, that she made her stage debut under the stage name of Dorothy Jordan. She loved musical comedy, and her favourite parts were those of tomboyish and musical and happy characters. William Hazlitt and Charles Lamb were ecstatic in praise of her. Lamb said that 'her child-like spirit shook off the load of years from her spectators,' and an unnamed contemporary critic said of her that she had the advantages of elegant and polished society, together with a natural cheerfulness of disposition and a highly accomplished mind. And it was at the Theatre Royal, Drury Lane, that she met William, Duke of Clarence, later to become William IV of England. They lived together as man and wife for twenty years (at times in Clarence House) and had ten children. She gave him much of her fortune and remained to the end intensely loyal to him. But William was clearly in line for the throne; the long and royal romance came to an end in 1814; and Dorothy Jordan, William's duchess, escaped to France. There, in July of 1816, at St Cloud, a suburb of Paris, she died, alone and poor and friendless.

Much that was inaccurate and contradictory was written about her during her lifetime and after, and in particular about her early years. Edward Laws, the historian, had heard that some of her childhood had been spent in St David's. A local correspondent, writing under the pen-name 'Dewi Penfro', stated in one of the contemporary English magazines that 'Miss Bland, afterwards Mrs Jordan, was born in Treleddyn and educated in a dame school in Solva.' But she did come to St David's, obviously to visit her brother and sisters. It was reported that Samuel Harries, the gallant 'Major' of Trevacoon, would send his coach and horses, the first in the parish, to take her for drives in the country. William, Duke of Clarence, also

111

came to Pembrokeshire. There is a delightful story, told in Phillips and Warren's *History of Haverfordwest*, of the Prince's stay in the Castle Hotel, and of how he ordered a pair of shoes from a shoemaker on Prendergast Hill. It took Brian Fothergill's biography of Dorothy Jordan (1965) to reveal that she was born in London on 22 November 1761 and baptised on 5 December, as recorded in the registers of St Martin in the Fields, the actors' church.

It was natural that Dorothy Jordan should visit her brother and sisters. But why did Nathaniel and Lucy and eventually Hester Bland come, presumably from London, to Treleddyn and stay there? The answer lies in family pride, marriages and inheritance and wills.

Thomas Williams of the parish of Whitchurch and Blanch Scudamor Philipps of the parish of St David's were married by special licence by Delabere Pritchett on 10 August 1758. Thomas Williams was a man of property, a merchant, owner of boats and agent of Lloyds. He became a Justice of the Peace and High Sheriff of the county in 1788. He was also the man who first spotted three ships and a lugger sailing under false colours to the French Invasion of Fishguard.

Blanch Scudamor was the youngest daughter of Thomas Phillips, gent, of Treleddyn, and Elizabeth his wife. Thomas Phillips died young and Blanch outlived her brothers and sisters to become heiress and owner of the big house. She died in January 1788, and Thomas Williams then married Margaret Theodosia, daughter of John Harries of Priskilly, one of the Harrieses of Trefacoon and Heathfield and Tregwynt. Both marriages were childless, and so Thomas Williams came face to face with the most difficult of problems: he had to write his will. His own estate he gave on trust to his second wife. His first wife's estate he had to dispose of according to the terms of her will, no detail of which is known except what is quoted in his will—

> ... the whole estate in the parish of Meline goes to Nathaniel Bland, one third goes to him on my decease and one third of Treleddin goes to Hester Bland his sister and on my present wife's decease the whole of Treleddin as my first wife desired by her will.

Thomas Phillips of Treleddyn was proud of his family. His gravestone in the cathedral yard bears the following words—

Here lieth the body of Thomas Phillips of Treleddin, gent, who was descended from the family of Cyffig in the county of Carmarthen, who departed this life January 30, 1728, aged 44 years.

Blanch Scudamor was her father's daughter. Her estate had to go to near relatives, people of her own blood. It went to Nathaniel and Hester Bland. Lucy Bland, the youngest of the Bland family, incidentally, had died in Treleddyn in May 1778, in the fourteenth year of her age. That was the year of Blanch Scudamor's death, and, significantly, they were buried in the same grave.

How were Grace Phillips and Blanch Scudamor related? Grace Jerrold's *The Story of Dorothy Jordan* (1914) makes them out to be sisters. The Phillips family tree disproves that. If not sisters, what then? The answer (or at least the most convincing answer so far found) lies in the family tree of Thomas Phillips of Treleddyn, Blanch Scudamor's father. This reveals that Thomas Phillips's father was Roger Phillips of Meline, and that his grandfather was the Reverend Thomas Phillips of the parish of Meline. And in a related family tree is the name of the Reverend Scudamore Phillips of Cyffig: which explains the reference to the family of Cyffig on Thomas Phillips's gravestone, and the reference to her Meline estate in Blanch Scudamor's will.

That family tree also reveals that Thomas Phillips of Treleddyn had a brother, George, and that he had three daughters, Anne, Mary, and Grace. Blanch Scudamor and Grace Phillips were first cousins. Blanch, wealthy, comfortable in her ancestral home, married but childless, had accepted her first cousin's children into the sanctuary of Treleddyn, and in her will had bequeathed her two estates of Meline and Treleddyn to Hester and Nathaniel. Dorothy was on the stage of Drury Lane.

Legends, naturally, gathered around this royal and romantic link with Upper Treleddyn. There is one fact of a footnote. When the royal romance was on, the three children of Dorothy's liaison with Sir Richard Ford were cared for in London by her sister, Hester. When William Duke of Clarence came to the throne he gave Hester a royal allowance. That allowance was continued by Queen Victoria till Hester's death in 1848. [The most recent biography of Dorothy Jordan, Claire Tomalin's *Mrs Jordan's Profession*, was published November 1994.]

113

Porth Glais

Porth Glais is best in winter, alone with its dark rocks and stones and red soil and heather and bracken, and water and changing sky, and a few tied up boats. It is then its elemental self, around it the ghosts of the past. There is nothing else, except a strange magic, and the stillness of elemental nature, no different perhaps from what it was in the time of the coracle-paddling Saints. Porth Glais in winter breathes stillness.

Spring brings a change. The flowers begin to grow, the gorse is golden in the sun, the reeds grow green and tall, and Porth Glais stirs into life. The boats and the men appear. There is painting and hammering and varnishing. Prows loom above the wild bushes around the boat park that once was a car park and before that a coalyard. There is anticipation in the air. Easter is on its way, and with it the commerce of the coast.

Porth Glais, like many other parts and parcels of St David's, is not what it was, except perhaps in looks. And why was it called Porth Glais, or Porth Glaish, as the natives call it? Some think that the name is derived from *clas*, the name given to the mother churches that developed from the early Christian monasteries. In other words, that Porth Glais was the *porth* or port of the *clas* of 'Chell Mwni', the monastery of David. Hardly. There is another and more natural explanation—in the word *claish*, which means a groove or cut or narrow valley, and a word that also appears in the many place-names of Western Scotland on the Celtic fringe. It is apt, a fitting description of the narrow snaky little cleft through which the river Alun flows at the end of its six mile journey from Llangidige Fach to St Bride's Bay and the sea. That was the way, through creek and valley, that the first invaders came into this land.

Not far from Porth Glais is the massive granite rock called Clegyr Boia, the rock of Boia. It overlooks both creek and valley, and hidden in its upper reaches is a deep depression, a bowl that was an ideal place for early settlement. Excavations have proved that two groups of early invaders made their home there, first Neanderthal or New Stone Age Man, and then the Irish Celts of whom Boia the chieftain and enemy of Dewi Sant was one.

114

What did Dewi Sant have to do with Porth Glais? One of the mysteries in the history of the Saint is that we don't know where he was born. Rhygyfarch's *Life*, written five hundred years after his death, does not mention the place. It was Gerald of Wales, a century later still, who rewrote that *Life* and gave details of birth and baptism and early miracles, and linked all those details with Porth Glais. And he could well have done it for his own benefit.

Following the establishment of the monastery and the spread of the cult of David, Mynyw (the old name of St David's) became a central point, geographically at the crossroads of communications with the other Celtic Churches of the Western Seas, and a centre of pilgrimage. Saints from all those regions came to Porth Mawr and Porth Glais, and it is possible that they preferred to carry their coracles along the Valley from one side to the other (if, for instance, pilgrims from Cornwall wanted to go to Ireland) rather than risk the dangerous currents around St David's Head. The Valley became a very important place, and those little landing places on either side.

Twice in a much later age Porth Glais became involved not in the pilgrimages of saints but in the noisier confusions of war. In 1081 William the Conqueror paid his surprise visit to St David's. In that same year Gruffydd ap Cynan, exiled prince of Gwynedd, landed in Porth Glais with a motley army from Ireland, intent on regaining his kingdom. There he met Rhys ap Tewdwr, exiled prince of Deheubarth (the kingdom of the south) and patron prince of the cathedral. They came to an agreement, joined forces, marched to the cathedral to get the blessing of Bishop Sulien (J. E. Lloyd has a magnificently clangorous description of this motley march in his *History of Wales*), and then went north to win the battle of Mynydd Carn that restored them to their respective kingdoms.

Less than a hundred years later the peace that is characteristic of Porth Glais (the lapping of waters and the screech of sea-birds) was again disturbed. The year was 1169. The little creek (hard as it is to imagine) saw the gathering of knights from the south of the county, relatives of Gerald of Wales, and all of them intent on assembling men and horses and boats for the conquest of Ireland. They went and won so thoroughly that Henry II had to go and keep them in check. It was then that he came to Penporth Gwyn and went to the cathedral with the procession of canons.

Vandalism and war have at various times marred and damaged the fabric of the cathedral, and it was in 1385, after a spell of such damage, that Hugh de Pickton became supervisor of the fabric, the work that as Master of the Fabric the dean carries out today. It is in his detailed record for the year that we find the name of Porth Glais mentioned seven times and the kind of trade that had passed through this awkward little creek. Timber and limestones, lead and iron and coal were brought in, all destined for work on the cathedral. The little harbour evidently was of use to the cathedral community, and on the basis of this alone there is no need to ask who authorised the building of the harbour wall. Certainly not the Romans.

Here then is evidence of trade, and it is with this trade, humdrum, limited but important, that the history of Porth Glais remained up to the 1930s, and to some degree afterwards. There was a significant development in the time of Elizabeth I. Trade needed expansion, coasts and waterways needed protection, and ports had to be registered. In one royal document Porth Glais is mentioned on seemingly equal terms with Milford

The slipway, wheels for boat transport, and the pub.

116

Loading of *Sultan* for Barnstaple.

Haven. Two boats were listed under St David's, each of eight tons and each with a crew of four, their owners Thomas Williams and Thomas John ap Philipe. Each traded with Ireland, and each went 'up Severne afishing.' And Thomas Perkins of St David's was appointed 'for the keeping and surveying of havens' from Solva to Fishguard.

Numbers and sizes of boats varied considerably over the years; most were between twenty-five and one hundred tons. Ownership, particularly in the nineteenth century, was corporate—a mariner or a master mariner, a merchant, a boat builder, and a farmer or two. Farmers were particularly fond of the sea; neither they nor any other dweller on this peninsula was ever more than four miles from the coast. Cargoes followed a fairly predictable pattern. Essentials were brought in, and some of the luxuries of living—wines, pepper, salt, and timber from Ireland. Coal was imported from Lydney and Swansea, and culm, and limestones from south Pembrokeshire. Lime was used for building work, for counteracting the acidity of the soil (lime for

117

George Owen of Henllys was the 'chiefest' help to improve the land) and for whitewashing houses and farm buildings inside and out. Grain was exported to the Severn ports, Barnstaple and Bristol, and to North Wales. Barley was a special and abundant export. Another was butter. And seabird eggs were sent to Bristol for the refining of wines.

Occasionally a special cargo was brought in. In 1743 for instance, essential building materials for the cathedral chapter house. Again cargoes of building material were brought in for Tabernacle chapel, the present chapel which was completed in 1877. When the Lifeboat Station at Porth Stinan was being built, the bulk of the stones were carted from Caerfai and Caerbwdi to Porth Glais and transported to the new site by raft. Strangest of all perhaps was the cargo of flour and meat that came in by lifeboat when, in March 1947, the city of St David's was completely cut off by one of the greatest snowstorms in living memory.

The writing meanwhile had been on the wall from the beginning of this century. Improved roads; the opening of the station yard at Mathry Road (a meeting in Mathry in 1870 began the discussion of a plan to bring the railway from Mathry Road

Porth Clais harbour, with lime kilns.

118

right into the heart of St David's, into New Street: the City Hotel was built to be ready for its trade); and the development of road transport following the introduction of the petrol engine: they all gave warning of the end of the old coastal trade. The last cargo of coal came into Porth Glais in the 1930s. It was destined for the gasworks, built in 1901 and sited on the boat yard of today. These gasworks are now gone. So are all the store buildings and living accommodation that were near the lime-kilns on the south side of the creek. The harbour wall has been partly restored; the limekilns (four in all, but there was a fifth at one time on private land above the culvert bridge) have been excellently restored. The not so old landing stage on the creek is still here. Nothing much else remains as evidence of a long and difficult history of a place that was once busy within its limits. And those limits were considerable: a difficult entrance, a narrow creek, no facilities, a backbreaking job loading and unloading between the tides. And outside there was always the fickle play of wind on sails and a most dangerous coast.

It was these that brought the lifeboat to St David's. The 'General Farrell' was for some time stationed in Porth Glais harbour and launched over skids. But tidal Porth Glais was no place for a lifeboat. It was moved eventually to one of the magnificent and sheltered coves on this coast, the narrow cleft at Porth Stinan, St Justinian's. Today the Lifeboat Station stands cheek by jowl with the roofless chapel of the Saint, where once medieval mariners and pilgrims made their little contributions in gratitude and in hope.

St David's has seen some remarkable changes in this century. Not that it is on its own in that. Most other coastal towns have changed. There was a time when every household in the city, or nearly every one, had some connection with the sea. The place swarmed with mariners and master mariners (in sail and steam), men in peaked caps, 'captains all', men who owned and loved their boats and loved the smell of the sea in their nostrils, and who knew, like Sidney Mortimer and Dai Lewis, the currents of the Sound like the back of their hands. They took their daily walk to Porth Glais, not along Lower Moor but along the old pathway past Carn Warbwl (Warpool Court), the old way. Now there are very few whose lives are directly connected with the sea. Notwithstanding, the lifeboat is still here, and coxwain and crew of six (it used to be eight), and a long list of volunteers in waiting, and the Ladies Guild in support. The Lifeboat Service is very important in the life of the parish.

The old lifeboatmen knew Porth Glais. They fished out of the little creek as their forefathers had done in Tudor times. In 1966 it was reported that the creek served one full-time and about twelve part-time fishermen catching shellfish and wet fish in season, in St Bride's Bay and around Ramsey and Skomer. They caught mackerel in season, and herrings. One old story, with a characteristic swipe at the church, said that the vicars choral in their one-time greed tried to impose tithes on the herring catches, and that the herrings went away.

Today fishing and moorings are controlled, the harbour is now owned by the National Trust, there is a harbour committee, and a harbour master (the equivalent of the old 'tidewaiter'). Organisation rules.

There are twenty-eight canopied stalls in the cathedral choir, and a richness of misericords. Only two show any connection with the sea; one shows two men building a boat. The remarkable thing is that the men of St David's throughout the centuries have shown their skill in handling boats, yet throughout a long history there has been no evidence of boat-building. The peninsula lacks timber. Upper and Lower Treginnis between them boast one tree, one ash-tree, sitting on the dividing hedge.

Islands

Someone has said of legends that to have known them is what matters. No questions should be asked.

At the beginning of Rhygyfarch's *Life of St David* is a little of the history of Patrick, the man who was destined to become Patron Saint of Ireland. In his wanderings he came to Vallis Rosina, which the Britons, says Rhygyfarch, commonly call Hodnant. He found it a very pleasant place and thought that he would settle and serve God faithfully there. Then the angel intervened and told him that the whole of Ireland was to be his mission field. 'At these words he raised his eyes from the place in which he was standing . . . and beheld the whole' of Ireland. That is impossible. Not even so large an island as Ireland can be seen from the Cathedral Close. He had that inward eye that could see visions and dream dreams. And see islands of the mind.

There is that story—Robert Southey knew it—of a certain Gruffydd ap Eynon who one day from the cathedral yard saw an island far out at sea. So enchanting was this gleam of an island that he straightaway went to his boat to get to it. But the nearer he got to it the less he saw and when he arrived there was nothing there. He tried again, this time—doing what he had been told—with a sod of the sacred cathedral turf in his boat. Again he failed. Then he was told that he should stand on that piece of turf in his boat. He landed safely, and was seen no more.

Islands have an attraction and a satisfaction of their own, and their own peculiar magic. They stand apart from the hurly-burly of mainland life; they offer their own peace, apartness, beauty. To Saints they offered the life of the solitary, the ultimate in sanctity. Brendan the Navigator mistook a whale for an island, and returned eventually to his monastery, full of knowledge that life after all is a voyage of discovery, a looking for a promised land. It was the isolation of the island that drew Justinian to Ramsey, and Cuthbert to Farne, and Columba to Iona.

The islands of the explorer and the mystic became the islands of myth and legend. The *Tylwyth Teg*, the Little Folk, lived on islands around the coast of Pembrokeshire. And it was in

121

Gwales, Grassholm in St Bride's Bay, that the seven companions of Branwen, daughter of Llŷr in the second story of the Mabinogion, sojourned for forty years, enjoying a lotus life, forgetful of all tragedy and full of a seeming youth, until someone opened the forbidden door and let in the wicked past.

These islands around the Head have their names, metaphorical and otherwise, have their own character, their dangers, and their loveliness. Some have names from the farmyard—in the middle of the Sound is Y Ceffyl (the Horse) and not far away Y Bedol (the Horseshoe). Horses sometimes cast a shoe. Some have their terrors manifested in their names—the Bitches, a series of jagged rocks, claimed the lifeboat 'Gem' and three of her crew in 1910. Some, like Carreg Gwylan (the gull) take their names from the birds whose sanctuary these islands are. Some, like the Chantor's Seat and Carreg yr Esgob (Bishop's Rock) belong to the cathedral.

Misericord—the cathedral choir. Four men in a boat.

Tide run through The Bitches. Scene of the loss of the 'Gem' 1910.

These are the small ones. The larger islands, Ramsey, Skomer, have their own literature in the writings of R. M. Lockley and Roscoe Howells.

These are our islands, always there, but not always seen, clear as etchings one day, blurred in soft mist the next, sometimes completely blotted out. Are we prepared to take a piece of the sacred turf from the cathedral yard and point our boat towards them? There is an alternative. Stay on dry land, go along the coast road and to the little village of Tretio. By the right-angled bend below the old deserted Baptist chapel, stop, and look along the low level line across Dowrog Moor, towards the cathedral and the south east. Perhaps a magic veil of mist will blur the outlines and merge the background of land and sea and sky into a blend of green and grey. But if things are right, when the bright air of this land glistens like a sheet of steel, then above and beyond the cathedral you will see, perhaps two, perhaps more, islands of magic beauty, suspended in an abnormal clarity above the tower of Bishop Vaughan. Magic is still around.

Islands are description and metaphor in one. They are 'gwerddonau llion', the green places of the sea, real and imagined. Were they the homes of the *Tylwyth Teg* (the fairy folk)? Or were they, as Robert Southey thought, the homes of the souls of Druids who, not having been Christian, could not enter the Christian heaven? We can make of them what we like. There was a tradition amongst the people of Trefin that the mysterious islands always lying towards the west can still be seen—from Eglwys Non, which is Llannon. Much depends on distance. Skomer, six miles beyond Ramsey, has a veiled beauty. So has Skokholm, another three miles out. Ramsey is green and lovely, and only a mile away. Enchantment calls for distance.

Ramsey

This two-humped camel of an island, Ramsey, is historically very much older than St David's. In the second century A. D. Ptolemy, Egyptian astronomer and geographer, marked Ramsey on his map and called it Limeneia, and that was long before our Patron Saint was born. The matter is easily explained. Seamen and navigators of old, with their small boats and sails and oars, never ventured into the open sea. They hugged and skirted the coasts and marked their maps with what they and others saw along the coast, islands, mountains, headlands. Somebody had told Ptolemy about Ramsey.

The name is said to derive from a corruption of *Hrafn*, a Scandinavian personal name, and -ey, which means 'island'. So does -holm, which fits into the pattern, because the adjacent islands, Skomer, Skokholm and Grassholm, are all said to have Scandinavian names. Richard Fenton knew that 'ram' in English is *hwrdd* in Welsh, so he called it Ynys yr Hyrddod (*hyrddod* being the plural of *hwrdd*). The Welsh call it Ynys Dewi, Dewi's Island. It is only a mile across the Sound, and did once belong to the bishop, but in 1905 the Chapel of St Justinian on the mainland and Ramsey were sold into private hands by the Ecclesiastical Commissioners.

The island's coastline is the home of the Atlantic grey seal that breeds in autumn, and of birds—guillemots, razorbills and kittiwakes. All these islands, Ramsey itself, Grassholm where 1700 pairs of gannets live, and Skomer and Skokholm, and the islands of the Smalls, are sanctuaries for birds whose eggs have in the past been regarded as rare delicacies. In 1964 it was leased to the Royal Society for the Protection of Birds, but this lease was not renewed when it expired in 1976.

The 626 acres of Ramsey have seen mixed fortunes, but in all the old documents, including *The Black Book of St David's*, the emphasis was on agriculture. The inventory of the goods of Bishop Thomas Beck (1280) casts some light on the early history of this farming. Goats were kept on the island, 70 of them, and 44 horned cattle. *The Black Book* goes further: it suggested that a hundred acres of Ramsey would keep ten horses, one hundred cattle, and three hundred sheep. These

125

Sphinx Rock.

sheep, according to a clergyman's letter written centuries later, had coarse wool, ran wild, and had to be hunted like deer. Strangely, the most recent experiment on Ramsey involved the breeding of deer.

When William Williams of the Grove (he died in 1899) farmed Ramsey large quantities of butter were made there. And something else. Richard Fenton tells us of Ramsey cheese: 'the herbage is very sweet, Dutch clover predominating over every other species of grass, intermixed with wild thyme: no wonder then that the cheese was held in great repute.'

One of the island's greatest difficulties obviously lay in the precarious and chancy links with the mainland—in the currents and submerged rocks of Ramsey Sound. Farm animals, for instance, had to be ferried over, and were sometimes coaxed to swim. This Sound (Roscoe Howells in *The Sounds Between* wrote of 'a raging white maelstrom where the waters roar ominously as they surge in their headlong rampage') has, more than any other factor, influenced the lives of those who have tried to make a living on the islands. Very few have succeeded.

Cattle, sheep, horses, goats and deer—from them to the most notorious animals of Ramsey, the rabbits and the rats. Ivor Arnold's diary (quoted in *The Sounds Between*) tells how he and his brother went out after supper to hunt rats; how rats and rabbits had nearly ruined the potato crop; how 'the rats are awful here now'; and how, after threshing all day 'the rats are by the hundred in the hayguard.' As for the rabbits they were at one time trapped twice a year; and five hundred could be taken without injury to the stock—a thriving trade that at times proved more profitable than more traditional farming. Most of them were sent to the coal-mining valleys of South Wales.

Ramsey is perhaps too near to the mainland to hold that mystery, that mystique that can belong to smaller islands. There is and has been too much business around it. Today most of it has to do with fishing and the holiday trade. But *The Black Book* tells us that, six hundred years ago, a ferry ran to and from the island, carrying beasts and all kinds of things. And in the days of sailing ships and busy coastal trade it was a short cut. 'The Sea-men thereabouts,' wrote Richard Fenton, 'made it their common Passage to and from North Wales, it being their directest route.' They paid, though, in terms of their lives. And persisted in facing the risks. David Evans of Twr y Felin, in the

127

early years of this century often saw between sixty and eighty of these little sailing ships going through the Sound on the turn of the tide.

David Evans bridged the nineteenth and twentieth centuries. It was in the days of the Celtic Saints that coracles came to Ramsey.

In the south-west corner of the island is Trwyn-y-mynachdy, which means the headland of the monastery. We accept the implications of such place-names as 'Parc y Capel' and 'Waun-beddau' on the mainland; then we must accept that there was once a monastic settlement on this island. Graves have been discovered on it. More significantly, George Owen of Henllys (and Richard Fenton) said that there were on it two chapels, dedicated to St Dyfanog and his fellow monk, St Justinian. There were other monks as well. Justinian and Dyfanog were Saints of Brittany and they had come to the island in simple craft woven of osiers and hides tarred in oak bark and rubbed with grease, searching for a solitary life. Justinian became the confessor of David, but, says the legend, there were enemies amongst his fellow monks (or were they his servants?), and they murdered him because his way of life was too harsh. His head was cut off, but he swam across the Sound carrying his severed head in his hands to fall dead and be buried in the place where the ruined chapel that bears his name now stands. His murderers were struck with leprosy and were sent to work out their salvation on Ynys Gwahan, which means Leper Island. But *gwahan* or the verb *gwahanu* also means 'separate' or 'to divide'. And this island does just that, it divides the fierce currents and tides of Ramsey Sound. Later, Justinian's remains were removed and buried in the same tomb as those of David, which explains why the remains in the sacred casket behind the High Altar in the cathedral are those of a tall man and a short man. Justinian was a short man, and David, says Rhygyfarch, was 'upright in stature of four cubits'.

On the spot on the island where fell the severed head of Justinian and on the side of the church that bears his name there sprang up those sacred wells so cherished by the Celtic Saints. Each had its magic power, conveying health of body to those who drank its waters. Sick people going there, said John of Tynemouth, after drinking returned home safe and sound, full of thanksgiving to God.

128

The Saints lived on Ramsey. But who, one wonders, were its first inhabitants? It has its Scandinavian name, but of all the islands across the entrance to St Bride's Bay it alone is distinguished by the fact that every geographical feature on and around it bears a Welsh name. Ramsey, yes. In more senses than one it is Ynys Dewi.

Most people today see it from a little distance, from pleasure boats making round-the-island trips. It is there, beyond, the island of three Saints, the island of birds and seals and caves, and sheer, terrifyingly sheer rock face. Are there any other tales to tell? There are, surmises from the past.

There is still no evidence that the Romans ever came further west than Carmarthen. Did they send their longboats down this coast and round Ramsey? Some say they did.

And the Viking longboats: did they hide behind the islands before setting out to loot and ravage the cathedral church? The answer must be Yes.

The laws of Elizabeth I were meant to guarantee supervision of the coast and stop piracy and strengthen trade. She appointed officers to do the work. Did they stop piracy? There is that marvellous story (culled by Major Francis Jones from the Record Office and recorded in *The Pembrokeshire Historian*,

The island from between Pencarnan and Porthstinan.

129

Volume 2). It tells of a strange ship in Ramsey Sound, of a Breton captain, of men from the crew scouring the island for sheep and cheese, of a gaggle of men from the parish, one vicar choral among them, and then the sudden arrival of a certain Thomas Williams of Treleddyn who had brought with him a couple of hens, a capon, a cock, which he hoped to sell, and a jar of milk which he hoped to trade for a bottle of wine.

Smuggling? There are stories of the big house of Treleddyn with its two cellars and the reputed tunnel to Porth Seli. Of course, there was smuggling here, and in Abereiddy and elsewhere, and the looting of wrecked ships (which Howel Harris the Methodist Revivalist condemned in the bitterest terms), and the gatherings of wreckage, and all the things that are traditional to a long and broken coast. Was it not all this background that gave rise to the once popular tales of L. A. Knight? Not necessarily the grim luring of boats on to the rocks and the looting of their cargoes, and the ravaging of bodies, as happened after the wreck of the 'Phoebe and Peggy' off Solva in 1773. Wrecking meant a constant watch on the coast and the harvesting of whatever the sea brought in. Every decent parishioner, from the most respectable farmer downwards, did it. The schoolchildren did it.

In the log-book of St David's Rate Aided School, dated 2 April 1874, is this: 'Large vessel wrecked in the bay. The neighbourhood has been wrecking all the week.' The children were granted a holiday on April 2.

Lifeboat

The old name for Penmaen Dewi or St David's Head was Octopitarum, which means a group of eight, the islands that lie beyond it. These are the rocks that preach 'deadly doctrine', said George Owen. He knew and thousands of mariners through the ages have known that there are other dangers in the westerlies and the southwinds. It is a dangerous coast.

Big ships and shipping lanes are now far out beyond the horizon, equipped with all the equipment and skills of this modern scientific age. There are still small boats around the coast. We still get wrecks. The lifeboat has been and still is the guardian angel of our coasts. But the days of sailing ships are gone. Their time of greatest danger, when casualties were heaviest, came in the great maritime expansion of the nineteenth century, and the explosion of trade between Bristol and the Americas. Multiplication of trade meant multiplication of ships. Richard Fenton saw St Bride's Bay 'alive with small ships in all directions', and Ivor Arnold on Ramsey used to count them going through the Sound. In two centuries, between 1750 and 1950, there were over one hundred recorded wrecks around this coast. Midway between those dates came 1859, the year of the great storms. In October of that year four ships were sunk around St David's, and eleven others off the coasts of Wales. The old church at Cwm-yr-Eglwys was destroyed, and the old pub at Newgale which was then on the seaward side of the road. Anger and consternation was widespread, people began to petition and protest and demand that something should be done. Too many lives were lost.

The lighthouse had come first. In 1775 a private licence was granted that allowed an open structure to be built on stanchions on the Smalls. It was a precarious affair, but it lasted till 1861. Then Trinity House took over, and the lighthouse that stands today was built, 145 feet high above the Hats and Barrels, flashing its three lights every fifteen seconds. The other lighthouse on South Bishop Rock, standing on the westernmost of the Bishop and his Clerks group, came into operation in 1838, on the Coronation Day of Queen Victoria. To the north is

131

(Top row): W. H. Thomas, Thomas Evans, Sidney Mortimer, James Thomas, Francis Rowlands. *(Bottom row):* William Banner, Billy Parry, George Martins, two unidentified survivors from the *Democrat*, James Williams, Brockus, Michael Moriarty. Three lifeboatmen were lost—John Stevens, Henry Rowlands, James Price.

The old Lifeboat Shed in Porthstinan.

Strumble Head Lighthouse, now automated, flashing its brilliant light four times every fifteen seconds.

It was almost a century after the first lighthouse was built that the lifeboats came. In 1869 the Lifeboat House on Trinity Quay, Solva, was built, and a lifeboat installed. In that same year the *Augusta* came to St David's, to spend some time under a tarpaulin in front of what is now the Old Cross Hotel. In 1877 the Solva boat, *The Charles and Mary Egerton*, was sold, and by 1879 a joint committee of the St David's and Solva Branch of the Royal Lifeboat Institution had been formed. *Augusta* was then moved to Porthlisgi, home of its first coxwain, David Hicks, and eventually found its home in the lifeboat station of today, Porth Stinan. It was followed there by the *General Farrell*, and then came the *Swn-y-Môr*, named after the home of Joseph Soar, Lifeboat Secretary and cathedral organist. The next lifeboat was named after him. *The Joseph Soar* then went to Scotland and in May 1988 a new lifeboat, *The Garside* arrived in St David's. It is still here.

The coastguards were originally under the Navy, but in 1922 they became a body in control of their own affairs, but still subject to change. George W. Manby, the man who wrote *History and Antiquities of the Parish*, invented the rocket firing gun, one of their early pieces of equipment, and stored then in the building that is now the Post Office in New Street. In 1882 Alfred, Duke of Edinburgh, came to St David's to inspect the tall houses that had been built for them. That was Royal Terrace. Then came the changes. Fifty years ago there were half a dozen coastguards in the city. Today one coastguard and one auxiliary do the job. The explanation is simple. The sea lanes have retreated from the coast. There is no further need for men to occupy the old lookouts, on top of Carn Llidi and at Carn Rhosson. The world is no smaller than it was, but electronic communication is rapid, reliable, and dispenses with manpower.

Lighthouses, lifeboats, coastguards, they are all on call to save lives. Long before the setting up of lifeboat stations there had been appeals that more should be done to reduce the appalling loss of life. In 1824 the Royal National Institution for the Preservation of Life from Shipwreck was formed. In 1854 all lifeboats, gear carriages and the balance of lifeboat funds were brought under one umbrella and transferred to this Institution, which was then named the Royal Lifeboat Institution. Caring

133

for those who were rescued was passed to the Shipwrecked Mariners Society.

All, men and boats and the backing organisations, have a very fine record behind them. And the support of the community.

A barometer stands by the Square. The coxwain of the Lifeboat, over the years, has made it his point to read it daily, and hardly anybody passes by without a glance. Why is it there?

The answer was given in a newspaper report of one hundred and twenty years ago—

November 1872
Royal National Lifeboat Institution,
St David's and Solva Branch.

The usual Quarterly Meeting of the Local Committee of the above Branch will take place at the Committee Room, St David's, on Tuesday, October 3, at 2 p.m. for the purpose of deciding upon a suitable place for fixing the Barometer which has been lately presented to the inhabitants of St David's by the Royal National Lifeboat Institution.

J. Rees, C. Browne
Hon. Secs.

Remnants of Industry

The story of old St David's, according to *St David's and Dewis-land*, is primarily the story of two communities, that of the Celtic farm and that of the church within the Close. They and their successors were the only employers of labour.

The *Liber Communis* of 1385/86 listed the workers who kept the cathedral in repair and put right the ravages of vandals. Over sixty names are mentioned, craftsmen, masons and carpenters, iron workers, as well as those whose job it was to fetch and carry. That labour force went up in times of restoration and extension; it fell when the church was impoverished and indigent.

City and country in the nineteenth century saw periods of prosperity. There was a vast increase in building work; increased trade meant more men going to sea; and there were more working on the farms than ever before. Census returns reveal a very wide range of craftsmen—horse riders, thatchers, cordwainers (shoemakers), weavers, blacksmiths, carpenters and joiners, masons, millers, bakers, coopers, slaters, lathcutters, molecatchers and cowcatchers; and washing women and quilt and bonnet makers. They contained the old country crafts; what the returns showed was the increased numbers practising those crafts.

Nevertheless, there never has been any other fairly large industrial base in St David's, nothing beyond the demands of church and farm. The only large single source of labour today is the St David's Assemblies that came here in 1951, a still thriving assembly plant of components that demands a substantial number of male and female workers. The only other industry comparable in size but not in nature was started in the early decades of the last century, outside the parish and on the coast road to the north.

There are two roads from the 'old' road past Rhodiad and Waunbeddau and Berea and towards the sea: one little side-road rolls down to slaty blue-black Abereiddy beach, the other leads to Porthgain. These two little villages (one thriving, the other silent and deserted except in summer) sit on either side of Trwyn Castell on the northern coast. *Trwyn* means headland,

and on it stands a *castell*, the remains of an Iron Age coastal fort like Castell Heinif or the cliff castle above Caerfai. They are two villages sitting on old volcanic areas that determined their similar and yet very different histories.

Abereiddy stands on an open little bay of that name (the little Eiddi stream runs into it), a sheltered bay, a slaty place. Once the beach was more slaty than anything else, but since the building of the wall against the sea in 1974/75 there has been a slow gathering of sand. The few remaining houses on either side are almost all holiday homes. On the north side of what is now a car park covered in blue-black Llanfirn shale there was once a 'row' or 'street', where lived a local clan working casually on the land and expertly as fishermen and poachers. That street was swept away when a violent sea came over the lot in 1938. There was once a pub there too, partly public but with another very private quarter where the natives drank their contraband. Smuggling was once a busy trade. Across the bay from the 'row or 'street' are a few houses, and over the hump and hidden are some others, and a stream, and a corn mill, now in ruins. And where the down hill road enters the car park there was once a flourishing garden, and limekilns, reminiscent of the trade of long ago.

Into this quiet world of fishing and poaching and casual working on the land burst the slate mining, no trace of which now remains but the long deserted buildings and cottages and slate walls that stand starkly black against the evening light. Slates from here went on the houses of St David's when the old thatch and zinc roofs were discarded around the turn of the century. These slates of Llanfirn shale (Llanfirn is the name of two nearby farms, but it is also an established geological term) also went up to the Bristol Channel and into south-eastern England. Compared with the slates of Snowdonia they were porous and poor in quality, which explains the frequency of grouted roofs in the parish.

This business of mining and exporting slates came to an end in 1904, after having endured a fluctuating market for between fifty and sixty years. It began when, in 1837, George le Hunte (whose family came from Artramont in County Wexford, hence the Artramont Arms in Croesgoch), married Mary Lloyd, one of the famous Lloyd family of Cilciffeth, and through the marriage came into ownership of a very large estate. George le Hunte

Abereiddi and 'The Street' before the 1938 disaster.

granted a lease to extract slates, flags and stones from two fields in what is now known as Barry Island Farm, land that lies between Abereiddy and Porthgain. The geographical nearness and their geological common base led to industrial co-operation controlled by local businessmen. Both places mined for and exported slates. But Abereiddy was under a disadvantage—it was difficult to lower the extracted slates from the high ground to the boats waiting in dangerous and open water. The result was the building of a railway linking the two places. It was built, and recorded on the maps as a tramway, about 1860, and its line is still traceable along the south face of the high ground, and it was along this tramway that Abereiddy slates were then transported to Porthgain, which had a quay, built about the 1850s and enlarged between 1902 and 1904. Later, when the bottom had fallen out of the slate market, this line was used to carry Abereiddy shale and waste to Porthgain, where, mixed with local clay, it was used to make bricks. These were used in the first place in the building of the extended industrial accommodation in Porthgain, in particular the crushing plant, and then they were exported on a large scale to South Wales, to the Bristol Channel ports, and to Ireland. It is said that many of the slums of Dublin were built from Porthgain 'seconds'. At their best these bricks, like the local slates, were not of a very good quality.

137

Later, when mining in Abereiddy had come to an end, local fishermen executed a striking finale—they blasted a passageway from the very deep Abereiddy quarry and let in the sea. The result was an enclosed and sheltered little harbour that, because of its depth and serene beauty in the middle of the slate remains, has been christened 'The Blue Lagoon'. Like the industrial remains, it is now one of the great attractions to summer visitors.

Porthgain carried on, despite trading difficulties, constant changes of company, and equally constant demands for modifications in building, machinery, and tramway layout. The United Welsh Slate Company of 1863 became the Porthgain Slate and Brick Company of 1893, and the Porthgain Quarries Limited of 1904. This was about the time that slate quarrying in both places came to an end. The brickmaking business was in some ways a side-line. But the company's motto was 'Economy', and slate waste could be turned into bricks. This ceased about 1878.

The company title of 1893 ironically placed the three products in their order but in geological reverse. The volcanic wealth of the area emerged first of all in shale that produced the slate; then that shale and shale waste combined with local clay produced the brickmaking material; but the area's greatest volcanic wealth lay in its dolerite, the hard granite rock out of which the headlands of this North Pembrokeshire coast had been made and whose hardness had enabled them to withstand centuries of pounding from the Atlantic Ocean. Crushed, this granite stone made excellent roadmaking material. And this became Porthgain's greatest and last export, coinciding, as it happened, with the development (in the early years of this century) of the internal combustion engine and the consequent growing demand for roadmaking material. To meet this demand the harbour was improved, the quarry and the railway systems developed. The Company built and ran its own fleet of steam coasters; sailing ships and powered vessels could now enter the harbour, with the result that vast quantities of crushed stone were shipped out—to the Bristol Channel ports, to Pembrokeshire ports, and as far as London; in June, July and August of 1901 a total of 13,000 tons. Some degree of prosperity had seemingly come to Porthgain, and it was this that made the closure, when it came, all the more shocking. It came, suddenly,

138

in August 1931, so suddenly, it is said, that equipment, engines, all working machinery, everything, were left abruptly there and then. The whistle went. The men went home.

Slate quarrying had completely changed the life of Abereiddy. Census returns tell the tale. Quarrying began in the early 1840s; the 1841 Census showed seven slaters in the parish of Llanrhian, two in Portheiddi and one in Abereiddy. A period of intense activity led to an invasion of slaters from outside, particularly from Anglesey. The 1851 Census showed that the population of the village had more than doubled; twenty-one were employed in the quarries and another five were dependent on them. It was at this time that seven cottages, two roomed and double-fronted and whitewashed throughout, were built by the company for their workers. This was Abereiddy's street. Young unmarried slaters came from North Wales, married local girls, and occupied these cottages. The place prospered. In 1855 the working of Abereiddy and Porthgain were combined, and the connecting railway began working. Demand for roofing slates was high—most of them went to Bristol—but the threat from North Wales quarries was already evident. In 1860 there was trouble. Products had to be pushed hard; third quality slates were offered cheaply; flooring flags were sold off at the lowest price possible; and slates were advertised as suitable for tombstones. Many can be seen in the nearby Baptist chapel at Croesgoch.

Th 1861 Census revealed the recession. The slaters from North Wales had gone; three of the cottages were unoccupied; and only the local families remained in Abereiddy, some of these being women and children only. The men had followed the slate trail. Abereiddy slaters were now working in Porthgain. There were company changes, though there was no sign of trouble in an optimistic brochure published in 1895. The slate quarry and the slab quarry were still working. The brickworks ('the only ones of the kind at work in the United Kingdom') were based on a profitable use of granite and slate waste material. The granite quarries had been provided with new machinery. 'A large trade was growing up.' By 1903, only eight years later, it was all over.

Linked to the industrial history is the social history, the background of the two places. Before the industrial invasion Abereiddy was a close little community. Then for a few decades

139

it became very busy, and then less busy. The departure of the slate quarrying threw it back into its original state. The flooding of 1938 killed it off. It now has a few holiday homes, an improved beach, and a quiet charm that is enhanced by the remains of its industrial past. And within its limits it is very popular with visitors.

Porthgain's history has been different. Apparently there was nothing much before the industrial beginning. It grew with the companies involved: it was a 'company village'. Today it is quite different, and has a charm that differs from that of most harbour villages. There is a mass of industrial remains, a fascinating piece of industrial archaeology. The little harbour is kept in good repair, the place is still active with fishing and pleasure boats. Nearby are the two limekilns, restored. There is 'The Green', immensely and artistically improved in recent years. There is its own peculiar street or 'row' of single-storey cottages, now excellently restored. Their weekly rent in the old days was ten pence in the old denomination, and twelve pence for some of the larger houses. There is 'The Sloop', social heart of the community, serving pints, they say, since 1743, and across the road is the Art Gallery. Those larger houses, once the homes of company officials, are all occupied. It is still an active community, so far completely immune to the threat of holiday or second homes. Porthgain is 'different'.

It is different and determined. In 1981 the villagers, fearful of speculators, clubbed together and bought the freehold from the company. The buying price was £55,000. The bill of sale hangs, appropriately, in The Sloop.

Saints Across the Water

That St David's and Armagh were confirmed as cities on the same day (7 July 1994) was no coincidence. That Rhygyfarch began his *Life of David* with a little of the story of Patrick was no accident. Patrick had to make room for David and move over to Ireland, which was Rhygyfarch's way of indicating that David was a greater saint than Patrick, and that Mynyw (this St David's) was to be the hub, the centre of the Celtic Church of the Western Seas. The Irish were already here, and their Saints were to cross the Irish Channel—at least their names and reputations did—as if they were citizens of one kingdom. The *Lives* tells us that Aeddan and Aelfyw and Declan and Finnian all came to St David's. And Aelfyw had a monastery on the coast of a lovely bay.

Richard Fenton knew that bay. One day he climbed one of the mountains of Ramsey, saw the seabirds, and the falcons so much fancied by Henry II, saw from there the panorama of sea and land, and looked east across the bay, and found it 'alive with small craft in all directions.' It is less active now. The little places on its perfect arc of a coast—Solva, Newgale, Druidston, and the Havens, Broad and Little—hibernate in winter and think of summer. It is a bay hooked on two points, Pen Dal-aderyn on the St David's side, Wooltack Point on the other. In between are the islands. And not far from Wooltack Point is a red sandstone cove and a church and some houses and an old limekiln. This is the village of St Bride's and the bay is St Bride's Bay. And St Bride was Brigid, the fine old Lady Saint of Ireland, St Brigid of Kildare.

Her father was a pagan chief, her mother a Christian bonds-woman who was sold to a druid who was later converted to Christianity, and at whose home the child was born. Brigid, whose name means 'strong', showed early signs of piety and strength of character, for she later returned to her pagan father, converted him, and persuaded him to help her with her work. He had planned to marry her to a king of Ulster. She refused, but her piety and beauty and persistence in the end made this king of Ulster grant her a great expanse of land in Kildare, and it was on this land that she realised her dream and built on it a

141

nunnery of great renown. That piece of land was called the Curragh. Today it is the headquarters of Irish racing.

That nunnery in the Curragh, perhaps the mother convent of Ireland, grew immensely in numbers and in reputation, so much so that Brigid called in a bishop to help with the organisation. And that led to a remarkable development. Next to the nunnery grew a monastery, forming a co-educational establishment where men and women worked alongside one another, the men developing skills in crafts, and the women, guided by Brigid, milked the cows and made butter, tended the sheep, embroidered and wove, and learnt the arts of housewifery. And that is why Brigid, adored by poets and smiths and musicians, also became the patron saint of the housewife and the home. Above all else, she was characterised by generosity; she gave to the poor and the needy all that she had, and all that was given her.

Did Brigid come to Mynyw? We do not know. Her reputation did. The bay belongs to her, and two other churches in Wales. There is St Ffraid in Llandysul, and on the Cardigan-Aberystwyth road is Llansantffraid, which is Llan-non.

Richard Fenton tells a tale about St Bride's, not the church in the village but an earlier chapel that had fallen into disuse and had been converted into a salting house for the herrings of the bay. That was sacrilege. The herrings went away. He had seen that chapel. It stood close to the shore a little raised above the beach, and there the fishermen put up their prayers for safety on the sea and for better catches. And there they were buried. Stone coffins, he said, were to be seen peeping out of the crumbling earth.

They say that the Irish recognised three orders of saints. In the first order were bishops, founders of churches; in the second, priests, founders of monasteries; and in the third, the holiest, were the hermits and the anchorites. Patrick and David and Brigid: they were the founders of churches and of monasteries. Govan was the hermit.

When and where the legend originated we do not know. Govan is a mystery. He was the lone saint who, like Justinian and Samson and many Irish Saints, left his land in search of a secret place where he could meditate and lead the life dedicated to solitude in prayer and abstinence and communion with his God. Justinian came from Brittany and found Ramsey. Govan

142

St Govan's chapel.

143

came, from where we do not know, and walked the high cliff edge of this county's southern coast and found a break and a rough pathway that led down to the edge of the sea. There, near the sea-washed rocks, he built his cell. Today, astride that path and some forty steps down, sits the little two-celled chapel dedicated to his name, built, they say, before the fourteenth century, and now restored. In the first of the two cells is a little stone altar and a dried-up spring. There, according to the legend, Govan lies buried. In the other cell lies the legend, or part of it. Govan was alone with his meditation and his bread and water, around him a silence broken by the screeching of sea-birds and the lapping of the waves. Then came the leathery groan of oars, and a long boat with shields. They, the 'gentiles',

Ynys Dewi and Whitesands Bay.

144

the Vikings had arrived. Fearful for his physical safety, Govan prayed and pressed himself against the walls of his cell. The wall opened and closed over his body, and there he remained, safe, till they were gone. Then he came out, and on that wall remained the marks of his body that with a little imagination we may see today.

Who was St Govan? A Celtic Saint, yes. Some believe that he was an Irish Saint adrift in Wales. There would be nothing odd in that. Others, fantastically, say that he was Sir Gawain, Knight of the Round Table, upholder of honour, who got tired of the Arthurian regime and sought to end his life in a religious way, alone. And that the retreat he found on this coast was first of all a cave in the cliffs.

This simple story of a Saint explains a place-name—the chapel was built long after the Age of Saints—and remains a wondrous tale. Between the chapel and the sea below was once a sacred well, like those of St Non in St David's and St Winifred's in Holywell, and the well near the now deconsecrated church of St Edrin in the parish of that name; all wells that were sources of miraculous cures. The waters of St Edrin's cured people and animals that had been bitten by mad dogs. St Govan's, like St Winifred's, cured ailments of the body, rheumatism included, which is why so many accounts mention crutches cast aside and left behind because they were no longer needed. Even as late as 1860, Murray's *Handbook of South Wales* said that St Govan's still attracted 'patients even of the upper class' and from far away. It still drew pilgrims seeking consolation of spirit and hope and relief from bodily pain.

These wells had rules. Why, then, had the waters of St Govan's Well to be lifted in a limpet's shell? That is the story. No harm can come from asking why.

Over to Naas

In 1991 moves were afoot that would lead to the twinning of the ancient town of Naas in County Kildare with St David's, then a city 'by repute' and in respect of its past, now officially a city, as is Armagh. In 1992 this act of twinning, of linking two places of different countries for purposes of special, cultural or commercial exchanges, was completed, signed, sealed, and delivered.

Why link St David's with Naas?

There are strong historical links. Naas, now a market town of 8,000 people, has been the administrative, law and order centre of Kildare since its foundation as a county. It has been built over an ancient site of great historical interest as its Irish names —Place of Assembly, Place of Assembly of Leinstermen, Place of Assembly of Kings—well indicate. To find the historical links with St David's one must go back to the twelfth century. In 1166 Dermot MacMurrough, king of Leinster, was thrown out of his kingdom, and crossed the Irish Channel to ask for help from King Henry II of England. What he gained in the end was the ear of Richard de Clare, Strongbow, Earl of Pembroke. Two Norman knights, Robert FitzStephen and Maurice Fitz-Gerald, became the allies of Dermot, crossed over to Ireland, and managed to help him regain his kingdom. In May 1169 Robert FitzStephen again sailed for Ireland with a stronger force that included Maurice FitzGerald and Meilir FitzHenry, and they were all sons by different fathers of Nest, daughter of Rhys ap Tewdwr, and uncles therefore of Gerald of Wales. With them also went Robert de Barri, who was Gerald's brother. These Norman knights and their men who sailed from Porth Glais on one of the most adventurous undertakings of the age were all Gerald's kinsmen, and in his book *The Conquest of Ireland* he calls them 'men of St David's'. They won land and power, and in 1175 the barony of Naas was granted by Strongbow to Maurice FitzGerald. This FitzGerald family became firmly entrenched in Naas and fully in control, and kept that control up to the time of Henry VIII.

In the centre of Naas is a Church of Ireland edifice dedicated to St David. Nearby is one of the many castles that stood within

146

Twinning: the commemorative tablet from St David's in Naas Town Hall.

the boundary, and this is called the Castle of David. The supposition is that the church in Naas, built on an ancient site of worship, was rebuilt in the time of William FitzMaurice, and that he, remembering all his family's connections with St David's (his uncle, David FitzGerald, was bishop from 1147 to 1176), not unnaturally dedicated it to David. It is also likely that this Norman knight, keen as all Normans were on building castles, was the man who erected the three-storey St David's Castle that stands at the centre of Naas.

So much for the history. Wrapped around that history is legend, the intangibles of legend, the stuff of hearsay and dreams of long ago. The first of many is that Patrick, having left Porth Mawr for Ireland, went to Naas, and camped on the green there. Did David go to Ireland? There was a time, they say, that he was better known in Ireland than Patrick, and that he had great influence there. He is often mentioned in the annals of the Irish Church. And didn't 'three holy men of Britain, Gildas and Doccas and David' take over to Ireland a 'missa', a mode of celebrating mass? One also remembers that sentence in Rhygyfarch's *Life*—that David and his three companions lit the fire of the Lord in the Valley of the Alun and that the smoke spread all over the country, and over to Ireland. The fact that

147

there is a church in Ireland dedicated to him is, however, no proof that he ever went there. Did the Irish come over here? Rhygyfarch says that the infant David was baptised by St Aelfyw, bishop of the people of Munster. His Irish name was St Ailbe, and that Irish name persists in Llaneilw, St Elvis, parish and church at one time on the coast of St Bride's Bay.

Dermot MacMurrough was king of Leinster. Ferns was the burial place of the kings of Leinster. And bishop and founder of the monastery of Ferns was that Aidan or Aeddan who, according to Rhygyfarch, visited David in the Valley whose other name was Hodnant. Aidan's name survives in Trefaeddan. Another name of his was Maeddog, and on the way down to Porth Mawr, alongside the road, is the sacred well called Ffynnon Faeddog.

Such then is the groundwork of this twinning, an intertwining of fact and legend, of religious contacts and influences, and facts of history in the form of Norman martial and political influences, a vast tapestry woven from the comings and goings of long ago, when Celtic peninsula and Celtic island were very much in contact: religious links going back over thirteen hundred years; and historical links of a mere seven hundred years ago.

Clegyr Boia across the moors from Rhosson.

148

Allied to this list of male Saints is that strong duo of female Saints: on one side of the bay St Bride, on the St David's side that of St Non. The two are drawn into an even close association, in Llan-non, and in Llansantffraid, on the Aberystwyth road.

There is much more than this to the Irish alliance. The Irish have been in this little corner of Wales from earliest times. There was Boia, the freebooter enemy of David. The Deisi came over in the fourth century and provided many kings of Dyfed. There are memorial stones with ogham inscriptions cut out on their edges, in Brawdy and Nevern and elsewhere, but surprisingly not in St David's itself. There are place-names in this parish of Irish origin, words like *cnwc* in Pencnwc, where *cnwc* means the top of a hillock. In comparatively recent times, in the 1870s, Samuel Williams of St David's demanded more police protection for the city: Irish gangs were working on the restoration of the cathedral. And one old St David's character, May Evans of Penarthur (she was over ninety when she died, and that was thirty years ago) remembered gangs of Irish people roaming the countryside and begging, driven out of their country by famine.

These Irish came, and came again, as they had done over the centuries. And some stayed and settled.

They are still here.

Yesterday and Tomorrow

Emrys Bowen wrote three books on the Celtic Church, and loved St David's. Professor of Geography and Anthropology at Aberystwyth, he was fascinated with the influence of geography on history. Those three books were on the Celtic Church and the movements of the Celtic Saints, and on the fact that geographical setting had made St David's the hub, the central point of that scattered seafaring Church.

Why, then, this little city here? Why a remote cathedral on a western coast? The earliest beginnings are easily explained. Men and women in the dim distant past came here looking for a new home. They came, and some stayed. They dug the soil and fished the sea and built homes and found here a wealth of stone and a great scarcity of timber. They built their homes and early farms where there was shelter and a spring or two. That was safety. They made their lives and much of that making was moulded by their new surroundings and by new invasions. They adapted to these surroundings and changed things as their knowledge grew. There was always change, and history and environment worked hand in hand.

This parish occupies the Dewisland peninsula, which is in fact made up of three peninsulas. St David's Head, Penmaen Dewi, is one, the others Point St John and Penmaen Melyn. They are three fingers stretching out to the Atlantic gales and into the warm air of the Gulf Stream. The climate, that is, is wet, windy, and mild. Soft soil washed away and eaten into over the centuries account for its bays and inlets. And everywhere, inland and on the coast, there are masses of hard granite rock that have endured glacial wear and the erosion of time and weather. (They say that on Carn Llidi can still be seen streak marks of glaciers as they slid down to sea.) The hard rocks inland are called *carneddau* (*carn*, a cairn), and there are at least sixteen of them within the parish. The hard headland of the coast is called *trwyn*; and these are clustered on the high ground around the northern and western sides of the peninsula. Along this high ground are old farms that were homes of the old farming stock. They lived there sheltered from the north wind, and looked to the south, and from their vantage points saw the more amenable and cultivable soils that stretch down to the shore of St Bride's Bay, and the 'trap land' of Penmaen Melyn, which, according to the 'old chronicles', was richly fertile and ploughed 'like a shingle beach'.

Why was it that these peninsulas were so attractive to the early settlers? They were accessible from the sea. They were remote, protected. They had soil that could sustain a living. They were new land.

The very earliest settlers came, not to these hard and rocky peninsulas, but to the softer carboniferous lands in the south of the county. Eventually came Stone Age Man in his log-hewn craft, and found Porth Glais, and then made for higher ground, to Clegyr Boia, and settled in its bowl.

The next group or groups of settlers came, perhaps four thousand years before the birth of Christ, and settled on all the lands around the Irish Sea. They were the early farmers, settlers who respected their dead and buried them under huge mounds of earth thrown over stone frameworks, skeletons of stone at which we look today in wonder, now that the earth has gone— Pentre Ifan, with its capstone and three uprights; Carreg Samson at Longhouse near Mathry; and the collapsed Coetan Arthur on St David's Head. All look down over estuaries or what once were estuaries; Pentre Ifan was once much closer to the sea than it is today. These same people also settled in Clegyr Boia, the Irish freebooter's fort, as part of an immense Irish colonisation of this peninsula.

The Bronze and Early Iron Age came about 500-400 B.C. These people, the Celts, came from the continent, not in a mass invasion (they were a very independent-minded people) but in families or clans that had once occupied all of Western Europe. They brought with them some basic language from which sprouted Gaelic and Breton and Welsh. They were good farmers with their iron tools; and expert at enlarging areas of cultivation; and they built their distinctive defences round their settlements. These were the coastal or promontory forts, made up of banks and ditches and stone-faced walls, all using the natural lie of the land. The St David's peninsula is rich in these: Porth-y-Rhaw near Solva; Castell Heinif; Penpleidiau above Caerfai; and (most significant of all) St David's Head with its Clawdd-y-Milwyr, the Warriors' Dyke, and the platform of round hut foundations and a small (Celtic) field system that is still

151

recognizable. Then along the north coast are Castell Coch, the Caerau forts, and Trwyn-y-Castell above Abereiddy.

As far as is known, the Romans, conquerors of the Celts, never came to this part of the world. The Celtic tribe that had settled here, the 'Demetae' (from whose name the word 'Dyfed' derived), was left undisturbed. It was when the Romans left that these western regions experienced a great change that amounted to a blossoming of Celtic culture and the growth of a Celtic Christianity that differed from that brought to south-east England from Rome. This was the beginning of the Churches of the Western Seas. Scattered as they were, they had to communicate across the waters. And the focal point of those crossings became St David's.

In the sixth century, we don't know when, Dewi came to the Valley, there to set up his monastery and to evangelise and revive a Christianity that the older Saints had taken into their monasteries and away from the people. The archaeological evidence for this earlier Christian Age is confined entirely to inscribed and carved stones dating from the fifth to the seventh century—those once in the nave of the cathedral and now destined for the Lapidarium; inscribed stones cemented at a much later date into the altar faces of the chapels; and stones carved in Latin and ogham or both that can be seen in churches not so far away, in Brawdy and Nevern, and further afield in Clydau and St Dogmaels. The presence of ogham is further proof of strong Irish influence; the Deisi, after all, had come from Wexford to settle in this land long before the time of Dewi, and they were to provide local chieftains as far ahead as the tenth century. The father of Non, they say, was one.

Last of all came the Normans, William the Conqueror first, then Peter de Leia, bishop, in 1176. Five years later the cathedral was built. These Normans reorganised the old Celtic Church; they made the cathedral their castle; and they won this land without striking a single blow. David had chosen this spot for its peace and remoteness. Rhygyfarch had written his *Life* in praise of the Saint and his Church. The Normans built their cathedral on the site of the monastery, partly out of respect, partly because they were realists skilled at turning things to their advantage. They won this Dewisland in the old cantref of Pebidiog through religion and not by force of arms. Bordering Pebidiog was Cemaes, and they had to fight for that.

Below St Non's chapel—bedhead, and a wheel of yesterday's hayrake.

153

Cathedral: heart of all the historical significance of St David's.

It was this rocky headland and the surrounding seas, the geography, and their influence on the history of the parish, that fascinated Professor Emrys Bowen. In this interaction lay the causes of all those changes in its history. Today there are skills and scientific discoveries and transport facilities that combine to liberate life and settlement and growth from those old limitations that geography had imposed. Today there are changes of a different kind.

In the coastal belt there is still limited and licensed fishing, but the coastal trade has gone completely—it is sixty years since the last cargo of coal arrived in Porth Glais. That coastal belt is now almost completely involved with the seasonal and holiday trade, and the local boats involved in that trade now tie up in both Porth Glais and Porth Stinan.

The city, more than ever involved in the service industries, has got rid of those blemishes that marred its image some fifty years ago—an untidy Square, dirty side streets, the open gutters down Goat Street. It is spruce and smart. And growing, although there is still no significant growth in the population of the parish. There are no crowded housing problems as there once were; housing sites have been developed under control.

Monastery to church to cathedral church: those thirteen hundred years have seen enormous change. In its eight hundred years the cathedral has seen medieval pomp and poverty, has been enlarged and vandalised and beautified, and been neglected and restored. It has in its function of cathedral its statutory services, day in day out; it has been the setting for great national and royal and innumerable local anniversaries and great occasions. And as a parish church it has to care for the spiritual welfare of its parishioners. As the 1993 address to the Friends of the Cathedral so eloquently expressed, a cathedral is more than a church. It is open every day; through its doors it welcomes all kinds of people from all over the world, Christians and non-Christians, people of all creeds and no creed. It is there to be seen and felt. Every cathedral has an atmosphere of its own, its *naws*. Or is *rhin* a better word? 'It gives us a sense of worship, beauty, order, space. People come because they are hungry for beauty, mystery and dignity', as they have always done. More than anything else, a cathedral impresses with an awareness of continuity, of things that stay and withstand the insecurities of time. The cathedral remains the one great attraction, the

155

continuity, the heart of all the historic significance of St David's.

The changes that most closely affected the ordinary everyday life of the people were those that struck the farms. They came quickly, and they hit hard. The probability is that they came singly and quietly: electric light for hurricane lamp; reaping machine for scythe; elevator for manual labour; a stable that no longer houses horses; fewer workers on the land; controlled working hours; the disintegration of the old family farm, agriculture no longer a self-contained and sustaining way of life, but a business open to the market forces of all the world. And another probability is that they had happened before the farmer and his family had fully realised what had struck them.

Some external evidences remain to reveal this past of no more than four or five decades ago. In the farmyard are those buildings built for a special purpose that is there no more. The old *llaethdy* or dairy had its slate slabs and troughs where milk and butter milk and cream and cheese were held and made. On the beams of the old kitchen, if it hasn't been modernised, may remain the vicious hooks where sides and hams of bacon were hung, salted and ready to mellow in the warmth of wood fires. It is only in the memory that the old routine of corn harvesting remains: cutting, stooking, airing, carting to the barn, threshing by whatever means, drying in the *odin* or kiln; ten or twelve operations all told that could, even in good weather, take as many days to complete. Today the combine harvester does it in a day or two with a handful of men.

Very few of the old farming families are still in occupation. Large farms have grown larger by amalgamation; only one or two of the traditional small holdings remain, worked by craftsman husband and his wife. Cereal acreage has been reduced; new crops, the gold of rape and the blue-green of linseed, bring more profit, subsidised. The milk trade is in process of change; the monthly Milk Marketing Board cheque was once the guarantee of stability and survival. Mixed farming has given way to specialisation. The early potato business lacks stability. There are more sheep on the farms, but the old pattern, where there were fifty or so on every farm, has gone. The woollen mills that worked the wool have gone. There are no working horses in the parish. And no more than two or three full-time farm workers. Machinery rules.

156

The old community of harvest is no more, for the farm has ceased to be what it once was, the home of generations of a family. The farm is no longer an integral part of the community. The continuing problems of agriculture are national and international. The changes of this century that they have brought on this parish were harsh and discouraging because there was and is so little else by way of work. The old farming stock had been the mainstay of the Nonconformist chapels. Those chapels now suffer from a declining membership and lack of that stability the old farmers gave. Almost all the old farming families spoke Welsh. Now the language is in decline. Then there is that other problem which is general and not peculiar to this parish—the young educated look to a wider life and for opportunities to better themselves and their prospects. When they can't get them here they go away. This leaves St David's, like other communities but perhaps more so, with a growing number of the retired and the elderly.

What can the future hold?

As Rhygyfarch knew that the Normans would bring change, so the Saint, five hundred years earlier, had known that change would come. Here is his last message to his people—

My brethren, persevere in those things which ye have learnt from me and which ye have seen of me.

The Welsh version of the Anchorite of Llanddewibrefi goes a little further

Arglwyddi, frodyr a chwiorydd, byddwch lawen a chedwch eich ffydd a'ch cred, a gwnewch y pethau bychain a glywsoch ac a welsoch gennyf fi.

Be cheerful, keep your faith, and do the 'little things'. That was the big order. We do not know what he meant by 'those little things'. We can interpret them as we please, but they must mean that in times of change we should hold on to some things that we have inherited.

City and parish have seen enormous changes in this century, let alone the past. It is nevertheless a city that has managed to retain a certain atmosphere, a *naws*. And it is this *naws* that drew the pilgrims throughout the ages as it does today. Ask them what that *naws* means and they will without hesitation

157

mention the clear and unpolluted air of this peninsula, and the peace and serenity of this so far unspoilt land and coast. They will mention the graciousness of the people. And inevitably they will mention the cathedral and the aura of sanctity that still lingers over it and its ancient setting.